Rachel Coyle is an experienced advocate and is regularly instructed in a variety of property disputes, commercial, landlord and tenant, land registration, adverse possession, forfeiture, service charges, enfranchisement, leasehold extension, rent repayment orders, right to manage applications, appointment of manager applications, beach of leases (leasehold), Housing Act 2004 appeals pursuant to sections 43 and 45, boundary disputes, tree preservation orders, enforcement of easements and covenants relating to land, trespass, unlawful eviction, injunctions, section 21 and section 8 notices, tenancy deposits, local authority connection referrals in homelessness, homelessness appeals and allocation, disrepair and anti-social behaviour injunctions and committals.

Rachel has completed secondments at One Source and Hyde Housing as well as previously volunteering in the procurement department of Stockport Homes. She delivers and assists with training at Inner Temple and with webinar and seminar providers across the country. She is a pro bono volunteer at Queen Mary, University of London Legal Advice Centre and trains students there. She has also taught Brazilian Lawyers on the Legal System of England and Wales. Rachel graduated with a first in Law from Queen Mary University of London and completed an LLM in American Legal Studies as a Draper Scholar at the College of William and Mary in Williamsburg, Virginia.

A Practical Guide to Hoarding and Mental Health for Housing Lawyers

A Practical Guide to Hoarding and Mental Health for Housing Lawyers

Rachel Coyle

Barrister, Inner Temple

LLB (Hons), LLM (American Legal Studies-Draper Scholar)

Law Brief Publishing

Published 2021 by Law Brief Publishing, an imprint of Law Brief Publishing Ltd
30 The Parks
Minehead
Somerset
TA24 8BT

www.lawbriefpublishing.com

Paperback: 978-1-912687-62-6

To my darling daughter Olivia who was born whilst this book was being written during the pandemic of 2020

PREFACE

This book is designed to bring together the different definitions and understandings of hoarding and the challenge it poses to practitioners.

It is intended that this book will serve as a helpful guide of the different actions that can be taken to deal with hoarding. Whilst various legal processes, statutes and procedure/s is explained, the golden thread throughout the entire book is:

a. no one case is the same;
b. each person is different;
c. assume other agencies do not understand what hoarding is so that there is no preconceived ideas impacting decisions made;
d. embrace a collaborative, multi-agency approach;
e. prevention is better than cure.

It is anticipated that the book will serve as a practical guide and individual processes can be understood against the backdrop of hoarding, as well as in isolation.

This book has been written and the law therein is accurate as of 31st October 2020.

ACKNOWLEDGEMENTS

I am grateful to my husband, Ben, for his patience and support while I wrote this book.

I am also grateful to my extended family and my clerks in Chambers for their continued support.

Rachel Coyle
November 2020

CONTENTS

CHAPTER ONE
WHAT IS HOARDING?

This chapter describes what hoarding is, summarising its key elements

In reading this book, it will be helpful to have a clear idea of the basics of what hoarding is.

What hoarding encompasses

Hoarding is the persistent difficulty discarding or parting with possessions, regardless of their actual value. Hoarding can be related to compulsive buying (such as never passing up a bargain), the compulsive acquisition of free items (such as collecting flyers), or the compulsive search for perfect or unique items (which may not appear to others as unique, such as an old container).

Hoarding can also encompass a specific habit such as the collection of newspapers or animals, but this should not be mistaken with collecting. In the majority of cases where animals are the animate object hoarded, they are found dead or severely ill.

In general, collectors have a sense of pride about their possessions and they experience joy in displaying and talking about them. They usually keep their collection organized, feel satisfaction when adding to it, and budget their time and money.

In contrast, hoarders tend to experience embarrassment about their possessions and feel uncomfortable when others see them, even though this may not seem obvious to the onlooker. They have clutter, often at the expense of liveable space, feel sad or ashamed after acquiring additional items, and they are often in debt.

Someone who hoards may exhibit the following[1]:

a. Inability to throw away possessions. The persistent difficulty with discarding or parting with possessions regardless of value is often due to a perceived need to save the items and distress is associated with discarding them;
b. Severe anxiety when attempting to discard items;
c. Great difficulty categorising or organising possessions;
d. Indecision about what to keep or where to put things;
e. Distress, such as feeling overwhelmed or embarrassed by possessions and, or alternatively, impair the social, occupational or other areas of the person's functioning;
f. Suspicion of other people touching items;
g. Obsessive thoughts and actions: fear of running out of an item or of needing it in the future; checking the rubbish for accidentally discarded objects;
h. Functional impairments, including loss of living space, social isolation, family or marital discord, financial difficulties, health hazards.

These symptoms often result in accumulation and, or alternatively, clutter congesting living areas precluding activities for which those spaces were designed, compromising the use of those areas. It is not uncommon for the affected areas to only be cleared and made cleaner because of the involvement of a third party.

The World Health Organisation ('WHO') finally announced recognition of hoarding as a disorder in June 2018. On 18 June 2018, the WHO released its new International Classification of Diseases (ICD-11)25. ICD-11 was presented at the World Health Assembly in May 2019 for adoption by Member States to come into effect on 1 January 2022. That definition is:

> *"Hoarding disorder is characterised by accumulation of possessions due to excessive acquisition of or difficulty discarding possessions, regardless of their actual value. Excessive acquisition is characterized*

---

[1] Frost R.O. & Steketee G. (1999). Issues in the treatment of compulsive hoarding. *Cognitive and Behavioural Practice*, 6, 397-407

by repetitive urges or behaviours related to amassing or buying items. Difficulty discarding possessions is characterized by a perceived need to save items and distress associated with discarding them. Accumulation of possessions results in living spaces becoming cluttered to the point that their use or safety is compromised. The symptoms result in significant distress or significant impairment in personal, family, social, educational, occupational or other important areas of functioning.

Symptoms and Mental Illness

Hoarding is a disorder that may be present on its own or as a symptom of another disorder. Those most often associated with hoarding are obsessive-compulsive personality disorder ('OCPD'), obsessive-compulsive disorder ('OCD'), attention-deficit/hyperactivity disorder ('ADHD'), and depression.

Hoarding is occasionally associated with eating disorders, pica (eating non-food materials), Prader-Willi syndrome, psychosis or dementia[2].

Compulsive Hoarding

Compulsive hoarding is

"(1) the acquisition of, and failure to discard, possessions which appear to be useless or of limited value. (2) living spaces sufficiently cluttered so as to preclude activities for which those spaces were designed; and (3) significant distress or impairment in functioning caused by the hoarding" (p. 341)[3]".

Therefore, there are three symptoms:

   a.   Excessive acquisition of possessions;
   b.   Difficulty discarding – placing of higher values on possessions;

---

[2]Hoarding has been observed in a number of other disorders including schizophrenia, anorexia, organic mental disorders, and depression.

[3]Frost R.O. & Gross R.C. (1993). The hoarding of possessions. *Behaviour Research & Therapy*, 31, 367-381.

    c. Clutter that prevents normal use of living spaces.

The causes of hoarding are not fully known. Some people start hoarding after a stressful change, such as bereavement or illness. It may be connected to a trauma, including as far back as childhood. Individuals that are reclusive or a perfectionist, may also be more susceptible.

Obsessive Compulsive Disorder ('OCD')

Compulsive hoarding occurs in 20–30% of OCD patients[4].

OCD is a form of anxiety disorder characterised by obsessions (recurring thoughts or images that cause distress) or compulsions (repetitive behaviours) or, both.

    a. Obsessions include fears of being contaminated by germs or causing of harm to oneself or others;

    b. Compulsions, on the other hand, can be acts or rituals such as repeatedly checking or washing and putting objects into order.

Hoarding is a sub-type of OCD. The cognitive-behavioural theory of OCD is based on the idea that distorted beliefs, assumptions and thoughts can give rise to feelings of anxiety and distress and if a person responds to these unpleasant feelings, avoidance and/or rituals build up over time.

This often means that hoarders (and particularly those with OCD) have:

    a. Problems making decisions – this includes deciding whether keeping something is of benefit or not;

    b. A tendency to be a perfectionist because whatever decision is made must be right but because this is not possible, for fear of the consequences, the object/s are kept, thereby avoiding the need to make a decision. Procrastination becomes commonplace;

    c. Emotional attachment – sentimental attachment is not uncommon even if the object/s in question appear to the onlooker to be

---

[4] Frost R.O. & Steketee G. (1999). Issues in the treatment of compulsive hoarding. *Cognitive and Behavioural Practice*, 6, 397-407

of little functional value. For the individual hoarder, however, the object/s may feel a part of who they are, their identity or provide them comfort;

d. Distorted beliefs such as feeling responsible for not wasting things and for using objects properly. They cannot bear to dispose of it because of the belief that they might need it tomorrow or some other day or time in the future, however far into the future that might be.

Can there be a pre-disposition to hoard?

Hoarding behaviour can run in families but whether this is genetic or a learnt behaviour is unknown[5].

It can stem from a loss of a loved one, loss of a pet, ill treatment in the workplace, to name just a few.

Physiologically, the regions of the brain associated with hoarding are the anterior cingulate cortex ('ACC') and associated areas. The dorsal ACC is associated with decision making. The ventral ACC concerns motional and motivational salience and experiences[6]. ACC activation is lower in hoarding individuals than in healthy individuals[7].

---

[5] Winsberg M.E, Cassic K.S. & Koran L.M. (1999). Hoarding in obsessive-compulsive disorder and related disorders: a report of 20 cases. *Journal of Clinical Psychiatry,* 60, 591- 597

[6] Grisham JR, Baldwin PA. Neuropsychological and neurophysiological insights into hoarding disorder. *Neuropsychiatr Dis Treat.* 2015;11:951–962

[7] Tolin DF, Stevens MC, Villavicencio AL, et al. Neural mechanisms of decision making in hoarding disorder. *Arch Gen Psychiatry.* 2012;69:832-84

CHAPTER TWO
THE FIVE MANAGEMENT
CONSIDERATIONS

This addresses the different methods of management and literacies, including what constitutes self-neglect

Multi-Agency Approach

A multi-agency approach is required to ensure information is properly shared. In doing so, there can be a proper assessment of risk and decision making that considers an individual's family history, their relatives' perspectives as to their care and/or wellbeing and the causes and meaning of behaviour. This encompasses adult services, housing services, children's services and mental health.

A multi-agency approach will bolster practitioner's resolve to support a hoarder with proper relational and emotional management.

A multi-agency approach will help practitioners to delicately balance prevention and intervention with one's autonomy and independence. The justification for both positions can be drawn from the European Convention on Human Rights ('ECHR').

When dealing with a case of hoarding, the five management considerations should be considered throughout one's dealing with a case of hoarding.

Relational Management

When speaking to a hoarder and/or having any dealings directly or indirectly with them, one should demonstrate that one is empathetic and have a genuine desire to understand the hoarder's backstory. This demonstrates a critical consideration of the value of what that practitioner is doing without undermining the autonomy and/or personal integrity of the hoarder. In turn, this builds a relationship of trust and confidence.

Interpersonal relationships and relational experience are key to success. Relationships are an important need of people. This is coupled with three basic needs: the need for survival and power, the need for social relationships, and the need for self-determination[8]. The focus, therefore, should be on helping people build their lives, helped by and through relationships with others. The focus when building that relationship is on 'health'. This is line with the definition of health by the World Health Organisation ('WHO') (1998). Health is *"a state of complete physical, mental, spiritual and social well-being and not merely the absence of disease and infirmity"*.

The availability of instruments to tap into varying resources in different contexts is important for early interventions to promote well-being focused on the individual[9].

One such model that can be adopted is the Positive Self and Relational Management model ('PS&RM')[10]. This defines a lifelong development as 'the development of individuals'.

Positive relational management relies on the ideas of care and respect of oneself and others, as well as the relationships between people. Positive relational management is fundamental to the development of relational and social skills including emotional intelligence and social support. With these skills one is more able to break any habit or tendencies to hoard.

---

[8] Blustein, D L, Prezioso, MS and Schulthesiss, D.P. (1995) Attachment Theory and Career Development: Current Status and Future Directions. *Counsel, Psychol,* 23, 416-432.

[9] Di Fabio, A, (2014a) Career Counselling and Positive Psychology in the 21st century: New constructs and measures for evaluating the effectiveness of intervention. *J Counsell.* I, 193-213

[10] Di Fabio, A and Kenny, M.E, (2016a), From decent work to decent lives: positive self and relational management (PS&RM) in the twenty-first century. *Fron. Psychol.* 7:361

Emotional Management

One should emotionally manage one's own stress and anxiety as it is oftentimes the case that the hoarder has a backstory as to why they hoard. It is part of a practitioner's role to carefully unearth the story that often lies behind the hoarder's behaviour. From there, the practitioner can consider what options or course/s of action are most appropriate for dealing with that individual.

A good toolkit, though this is by no means prescriptive, is:

    a. Learn to quickly relieve stress:
        i.   Talk face-to-face;
        ii.   Exercise;
        iii. Yoga;
        iv. Walk;
        v.   Take a deep breath;
        vi. CBT.
    b. Build emotional intelligence:
        i.   Social awareness – recognise and read emotions and how they affect one's behaviour and thoughts;
        ii.   Relationship management – as above;
        iii. Self management – control impulsive feelings and take the initiative.
    c. Meditation to tame:
        i.   One's distraction from obsessive thoughts and addictive behaviours;
        ii.   Hiding or covering of one's insecurities;
        iii. Obsessive thoughts and addictive behaviours.

Separation Management

One should emotionally separate oneself from the hoarder's story and/or situation.

<u>Organisational Management</u>

One should be sharing information when properly engaging in a multi-agency approach. In doing so, the practitioner demonstrates that they understand accountability whilst also weighing all the options available when dealing with a case of hoarding.

<u>Ethical Management</u>

One should not be afraid to challenge decision making that undermines a culture, race, religion, disability, or any other protected characteristic/s. This promotes trust and integrity. These factors contribute to the functioning and success of an organisation dealing with individuals that display hoarding tendencies.

Therefore, it is key for practitioners to be aware of not only the legal but also none-legal options and requirements to ensure that the work they undertake when dealing with a hoarder is affective. This includes drawing on relational, emotional and organisational skills.

The best framework to adopt is 'REMTIC':

    a. Recognise the issue;
    b. Evaluate alternative response/s to such issue(s);
    c. Make a decision;
    d. Test it;
    e. Implement it; and
    f. Collect the facts.

It might be considered sensible to implement an ethics programme:

    a. Provide practitioners guidance;
    b. Guard the organisation's reputation;
    c. Reduce operational risks;
    d. Create a consistent culture;

The focus, therefore, should be on increasing awareness and encouraging healthy practises amongst practitioners.

Self-Neglect

Self-neglect is intertwined with hoarding. There has been research evidence and published Serious Case Reviews ('SCRs') and Safeguarding Adults Reviews ('SARs') that have sought to highlight the tension between an individual's interests and those of others. Inevitably, this raises ethical and legal dilemmas about what constitutes or should be considered the appropriate duty of care and at what stage should an individual or organisation step in without infringing on one's privacy, right to family life and/or autonomy.

Self-neglect has been considered as a form of abuse and neglect by the Department of Health when drafting the Care Act 2014. This has not been considered in such terms in other safeguarding and/or protection services and/or provisions. The policy and legislative differences have depended on whether interventions are codified in civil and criminal law or adult safeguarding powers and/or duties.

Therefore, it is key for practitioners to be aware of not only the legal but also none-legal options and requirements to ensure that the work they undertake when dealing with a hoarder is affective. This includes drawing on relational, emotional and organisational skills.

What is self-neglect?

In the 4th century BC, Diogenes, a Greek philosopher, talked of self-sufficiency and freedom from social norms in life. The Greek word, sylloge, means to collect so the term *syllogmania* is often used to describe a form of hoarding where one compulsively hoards a variety of objects but particularly rubbish. 'Diogenes Syndrome,' therefore, has become the term used to describe a condition of extreme self-neglect, social withdrawal and apathy and a tendency to hoard[11].

Self-neglect even goes so far as including 'service refusal'. This is where those who self-neglect refuse services designed to relieve them of stress,

---

[11] Clark A.N.G., Mankiken G.D. & Gray I. (1975). Diogenes syndrome: a clinical study of gross neglect in old age. *The Lancet*, 1 (7903), 366- 368

bereavement or physical infirmity. Such services include meals on wheels, house cleaning or talking services.

Self-neglect covers bodily hygiene, failure or refusal to observe important health behaviours, and hoarding of objects or animals. Sometimes these overlap and an individual's case concerns more than one. These have been the focus of studies[12] and the Care Act 2014 statutory guidance.

One might self-neglect due to poor physical and/or mental and/or emotional health. It is not unusual to find self-neglect resulting from either unwillingness or inability to self-care. This may be wrongly perceived to be a lifestyle choice without proper and due regard given to why one has felt unwilling in the first place. Any organisation dealing with a hoarder should not adopt the approach coined 'professionals hid[ing] behind the principle of choice[13].'

Those involved with hoarders, whilst being trained on and made aware of psychotic illness that may be a cause or aggravating feature in one's hoarding habits and/or behaviour, should not immediately jump to treating the underlying psychotic illness and be led to believe a cure or control of such an illness will cure and/or control the hoarding. Even if treatment is helpful of that psychotic illness, it is likely to be refused and easy access to help, encouragement and working alongside friends and families is more effective[14], though not in lieu of appropriate talking therapy, CBT and/or counselling.

Interplay between the different literacies

The differing legislative and policy differences is why legal literacy is important. The European Convention of Human Rights triggers a tussle

---

[12] Braye, S., Orr, D., and Preston-Shoot, M. (2011) *Self-Neglect and Adult Safeguarding: Findings from Research.* London: SCIE

[13] Pritchard, J. (2001) 'Neglect: Not Grasping the Nettle and Hiding Behind Choice.' In J. Pritchard (ed.) *Good Practice with Vulnerable Adults. London:* Jessica Kingsley Publishers

[14] Wrigley M. & Cooney C. (1992). *Diogenes syndrome – an Irish series.* Irish Journal of Psychological Medicine, 9, 37-41

between autonomy and intervention when dealing with prevention versus early intervention and protection.

When faced with the question of intervention or prevention, one should not take a person's apparent unwillingness at face value without discussing the reasons with them and what they perceive to be their options. It is important for practitioners to consider the person's own perspectives and allow them the opportunity to explore with a practitioner's assistance their reasons. It is about putting the person's perspective at the centre, not that of services. This creates the much-needed relationship of trust.

This does not mean to say that practitioners ignore the risks but consider consensual ways of working towards a resolution and permanent solution to one's hoarding. This does not mean that practitioners should not ask questions providing it is asked in such a way as to show a respectful curiosity. This is where relational, emotional, ethical and knowledge literacy comes into play.

Drawing on these literacies, practitioners are better able to reach decisions whilst allowing the hoarder to feel that they are in control of the situation but without the practitioner losing sight of the core values. This removes any tension and lowers those risk factors.

Each person is different, and each person's needs will require a person-centred approach, not a general rubric or formula. Approaching one's self-neglect and hoarding in this way will enable that person to develop coping strategies at their own pace whilst allowing for transparency and sensitivity. This does not mean that the practitioner abandons a suitable timescale, but this should be considered in balance with what the law requires and engage with the individual with a coordinated multi agency method of working.

Admittedly, negotiating agreements and coordinating between different agencies involves various challenges:

a. Health and Social Care working with Housing;
b. Environmental Protection working with Housing;
c. Fire Services working with Environmental Protection and Housing.

The web grows and develops in such a way that often more than several agencies are involved but each has their own policy/ies in place. Where at all possible, agencies should attempt to streamline their policies between them when dealing with hoard to ensure consistency for the individual. Any lack of awareness of interprofessional referrals, communication or discussion interferes with the integration of agency efforts[15].

This is where organisational literacy plays an important role in ensuring that agencies and practitioners familiarise themselves with the roles of others and work towards the same end goal and care plan.

Legal powers – Generally

The European Convention of Human Rights (integrated by the Human Rights Act 1998) is not where the respect for one's autonomy derives. It can be traced as far back as the Magna Carta in the UK.

There is a difficult balance between Article 8 (right to respect for private and family life) and Article 5 (the right to liberty and security of the person) in matters such as where one is hoarding but the hoarding is attracting, for example, vermin which in turn impact neighbours and those living near to the hoarder. The neighbours would likely wish to engage their Article 8 rights while the hoarder would likely wish to engage their Article 5 rights.

On the mental health and care side of the law, there is the Mental Capacity Act 2005 and the Care Act 2014. There is a tussle between the respect for privacy, and support for people to make their own decisions, and stepping in when the hoarder is regarded to not, objectively speaking, be acting in their own or other's best interests. Intertwined with the legal powers thereto, is the desire to protect and maintain one's dignity whilst at the same time protecting them from harm (whether from and/or of themselves) and that of preventing harm to others.

---

[15] Braye, S., Orr, D, and Preston-Shoot, M. (2014) *Self-Neglect Policy and Practice: Building an Evidence Base for Adult Social Care.* London: SCIE.

Typically, the greater the risk to others from an individuals' hoarding, the more likely that intervention will be called upon, and would be regarded as reasonable and proportionate.

When considering hoarding and self-neglect, therefore, one needs to not merely cite the law verbatim but to engage with the moral dilemmas with a sound understanding of the law, promotion of human rights, engagement and ethics.

CHAPTER THREE
IMPACT OF HOARDING

This considers the impact different members of the family and in particular, children and what options are available when dealing with children

For those family members living with a person that hoards, living among the extreme clutter can cause physical and emotional difficulties. These difficulties can also impact those not living with the hoarder. It is not uncommon for there to be friction and tension. Feelings of helplessness, frustration, anger and even abandonment are just some of the descriptors used by those impacted by the hoarder's behaviour.

Family Conflict

The conflict that often arises concerns:

    a. the loss of usable living space, particularly the common areas like the kitchen, living room and dining areas;

    b. the financial strain whereby excessive shopping leads to debt and/or the maxing out of credit. This then has the knock-on effect of preventing such credit to be used elsewhere such as for the maintenance of the home;

    c. the inability to clean without being chastised for doing so. If one cleans or organises the home without the prior approval of the hoarder, the hoarder will feel deceived and learn not to trust their family (or friends) that they live with;

    d. control over parts of the home the hoarder deems as theirs. The hoarder tends to control how the space is used and does not let others make decisions about the home and/or that part of the home.

Adult Children

Adult children often have a strained relationship with a parent who is a hoarder. Over time the adult child may become estranged from their parent due to disagreements about hoarding and/or the adult child feels compelled to leave because they have no space and/or their relationship with their parent/s has become so toxic that they feel they have to leave.

Parents with young children may be concerned about their safety in a grandparent's home that is heavily cluttered. Over time, this means that grandparents may become more isolated and kept at a distance from their grandchildren. The grandparent-grandchild bond can also be damaged.

Caregiver Burden

Adult children of those that hoard may experience what is coined the 'caregiver burden'. This is experienced in situations where people are required to provide emotional or practical care for another person. It is the stress which is perceived by due to the home care situation. This subjective burden is one of the most important predictors for negative outcomes.

Being in the caregiver role may cause:

    a.   increased interpersonal conflict;
    b.   anxiety;
    c.   depression;
    d.   inability to cope;
    e.   loss of self-esteem;
    f.   loss of hope;
    g.   loss of a sense of security;
    h.   financial difficulties.

Partners of those who hoard

Whilst partners and spouses may put up with the hoarding behaviour at first, over the years they may not tolerate it any longer and it becomes the straw that finally breaks the camel's back in other argument/s that couple may have that has nothing to do with the hoarding per se.

Frustration and hostility build up, particularly if the hoarder has been told several times over to attempt to move their belongings. Sometimes it becomes so bad that couples divorce or separate.

If there are children a custody battle then becomes the battleground for a couple where one seeks to argue that the other has an unsafe home for the child due to their hoarding.

Health and Safety at Home

The safety and health of families is often put into jeopardy as a result of hoarding:

a. clutter means that it is difficult to clean and dust;
b. where dust accumulates and/or animal hair/s, pollen, mould etc, headaches, breathing problems and such like can become problematic;
c. Spilled liquids lead to mildew and fungus or unwanted pests.;
d. The inability to clean renders common areas like a kitchen or bathroom unfunctional;
e. Hygiene is not considered important;
f. Clutter means there is also a greater fire hazard (and even greater still if what is kept is highly flammable). Fire is especially a risk when paper items are piled high and located near the stove, heaters, or other flammable materials;
g. Clutter means that there is no safe exit route in the event of a fire. If paths are created through the clutter they may become blocked by falling items. If one lacks mobility this is an even greater danger;
h. If one has pets or is hoarding animals, the animal/s may not be able to access the litter tray/s and instead defecates inside the home. This attracts fungus, mildew and pests like rats, cockroaches and flies. In time it can become uninhabitable according to public health standards.

How young children may feel

The impact on young children is often forgotten. They may be young and still minors but the clutter (and the reason/s for the clutter) can stun their development and ability to create relationships and/or how they carry themselves socially:

a. They are embarrassed about having friends coming to the home. They may be bullied about this at school. They may be seen as unwelcoming by their peers. In turn, the child is led to feel isolated and helpless which over time turns into resentment;

b. If the hoarding is extreme, it might be that the child cannot study or play (both being important to their development) because there is simply no space to. This can impact their education and create long lasting damage as a result. In such situations, practitioners are encouraged to consider exercising and/or engaging child protection services;

c. Children may feel resentful, depressed, and/or angry about:
  i. 'sacrifices' they are expected to make in accommodation;
  ii. their parent appearing to value their possessions more than them;
  iii. feeling like they have to pick a parent over the other when there is a conflict;
  iv. being removed from the home if social services step in.

Legal Powers relating to young children

The Department for Education ('DfE') is responsible for child protection in England. It sets out policy, legislation and statutory guidance.

Local safeguarding partners and agencies are responsible at a local level for child protection policy, procedure and guidance but their powers come from statute. The three statutory safeguarding partners at a local level are:

a. the local authority;
b. the clinical commissioning group;

c. the police.

A multi-agency approach and regard for the five management considerations is crucial to the effectiveness of any intervention (or prevention). Pursuant to section 10 of the Children Act 2004, the local authority is responsible for promoting inter-agency co-operation to improve the welfare of all children.

A child centred approach is encouraged by three fundamental legal provisions.

The Children Act 1989

This requires local authorities to give due regard to a child's wishes when determining what services to provide under section 17 and before making decisions about action to be taken to protect individual children under section 47.

These duties concern children who are, or may be, looked-after (section 22(4)), including those who are provided with accommodation under section 20 and children taken into police protection (section 46(3)(d)).

Social workers have specific roles and responsibilities to lead the statutory assessment of children in need (section 17, Children Act 1989) and to lead child protection enquiries (section 47, Children Act 1989). Social workers must be supported through effective supervision arrangements as defined under the National Assessment and Accreditation system. Designated Principal Social Workers have a key role in developing the practice and the practice methodology that underpins direct work with children and families.

The Equality Act 2010

Local authorities defined as 'public' are to have due regard to the need to eliminate discrimination and promote equality of opportunity. In practice this means that when identifying needs and risks faced by each and every child assessed, no child or group of children must be treated any less favourably than others when determining who has access to services

The United Nations Convention on the Rights of the Child (UNCRC)

This international agreement provides a child centred framework for the development of services to children. This was ratified in 1991 by the UK.

Early Assessment

Early help assessment is encouraged. This should be done within a structured, evidence-based framework. Local areas should have a comprehensive range of effective, evidence-based services in place to address assessed needs early. Practitioners should share information as early as possible to help identify, assess and respond to risks or concerns about the safety and welfare of children.

If there are more complex needs, help may be provided under section 17 of the Children Act 1989 (children in need). Where there are child protection concerns (reasonable cause to suspect a child is suffering or likely to suffer significant harm) local authority social care services must make enquiries and decide if any action must be taken under section 47 of the Children Act 1989.

Statutory services include:

    a. section 17 of the Children Act 1989 (children in need);

    b. section 47 of the Children Act 1989 (reasonable cause to suspect a child is suffering or likely to suffer significant harm);

    c. section 31 of the Children Act 1989 (care and supervision orders);

    d. section 20 of the Children Act 1989 (duty to accommodate a child).

How to determine a child in need – section 17

Under the Children Act 1989, local authorities are required to provide services for children in need for the purposes of safeguarding and promoting their welfare.

Local authorities should undertake assessments of the needs of individual children and must give due regard to a child's age and understanding. Good assessments support practitioners to understand whether a child has needs relating to their care or a disability and/or is suffering or likely to suffer significant harm:

a. the assessment must be informed by the views of the child as well as the family;
b. children should be seen alone;
c. a child in need is defined under the Children Act 1989 as a child who is unlikely to achieve or maintain a reasonable level of health or development, or whose health and development is likely to be significantly or further impaired, without the provision of services; or a child who is disabled.
d. children in need may be assessed under section 17 of the Children Act 1989 some children in need may require accommodation because:
    i. there is no one who has parental responsibility for them;
    ii. they are abandoned.

Reasonable cause to suspect a child is suffering – section 47

Under section 47 of the Children Act 1989, where a local authority has reasonable cause to suspect that a child (who lives or is found in their area) is suffering or is likely to suffer significant harm on completing an assessment, it has a duty to make such enquiries as it considers necessary to decide whether to take any action to safeguard or promote the child's welfare. The section 47 inquiry is used to decide whether and what type of action is required to safeguard and promote the welfare of a child who is suspected of or likely to be suffering significant harm.

With disabled children, a local authority must carry out an assessment under section 17ZD of the Children Act 1989, and for young carers, section 17A. The Young Carers' (Needs Assessment) Regulations 2015 require local authorities to look at the needs of the whole family.

When parenting is not improving after early intervention and engagement has been attempted, then a legal planning meeting, in addition to an initial child protection conference, should be held. The meeting should be used as a time to gauge what is in the best interests of the child and where possible develop a child protection plan and, where hoarding is concerned, consider whether the hoarding can be dealt with another way such as legal action like an injunction or an environmental health notice, or whether the hoarding is so bad that immediate proceedings and exercise of powers pursuant to an Emergency Protection Order be carried out.

Hoarding typically triggers the need for a mental capacity assessment to be carried out on the hoarding individual. It is at this meeting that documentation relevant to a parent's capacity will become relevant including whether they have the capacity to litigate.

Proceedings can be avoided if parents are able to demonstrate their capability to safeguard the child by working with relevant services to improve and/or agreeing to a protective placement for the child, with relatives or under section 20 of the Children Act 1989 (provision of accommodation for children).

Housing practitioners play a crucial role in securing the evidence from the provision of accommodation and state of it which helps social workers to assess whether a parent is capable of looking after their child, even with their hoarding.

Care and Supervision Orders

Section 31 of the Children Act 1989 requires any application relating to the safeguarding of the child to include evidence such as this in addition to assessments made by the social worker as described before concerning the child's needs (and wishes).

Under section 31 of the Children Act 1989, on the application of any local authority or authorised person (such as the NSPCC), the court may make a care order or a supervision order.

A care order:

a. the local authority provides accommodation to the child to maintain and safeguard them and promote their welfare;

b. gives the local authority parental responsibility for the child and the power to determine the extent to which the child's parents and others with parental responsibility may exercise their responsibility,

c. is automatically discharged by the making of a special guardianship order or a child arrangements order dealing with the living arrangements of a child. It is only suspended but not discharged by the making of a placement order;

d. the order ceases to have effect at the age of eighteen.

A supervision order:

a. places the child under the supervision of a designated local authority;

b. can limit what activities the child can engage in and/or requires the child to report to a particular place at certain times/days.

If the court is satisfied, then it will apply the welfare checklist at section 1(3) of the Children Act 1989 and the 'no order' principle set out at section 15 of the Children Act 1989.

A placement order:

a. Pursuant to section 21 of the Adoption and Children Act 2002, the court may make such an order that permits the local authority to place a looked after child for adoption.

When dealing with such orders, the courts must deal with the case within 26 weeks pursuant to section 32 of the Children Act 1989. When considering the order to be made the court will have regard for any care plans. Where hoarding is the precipitator, this will involve housing practitioners assessing their stock when being asked to potentially provide temporary or other accommodation to and/or for a child, considering the extent of the hoarding and what powers it has exhausted to date.

Interim orders can be obtained but should only be made if there are reasonable grounds for believing that the threshold test in section 31(2) has been met. The welfare checklist is considered by the court pursuant to section 1(3) as is the no order principle at section 1(5).

Duty to Accommodate – section 20

Under section 20 of the Children Act 1989, the local authority has a duty to accommodate such children in need in their area when assessing children in need and providing services, specialist assessments may be required.

Immediate harm

Emergency Protection Order ('EPO')

Where there is a risk to the life of a child or a likelihood of serious immediate harm, local authority social workers, the police or NSPCC should use their statutory child protection powers to act immediately to secure the safety of the child. It is not uncommon for housing practitioners to be the first to detect serious harm.

Sometimes, it is necessary to remove a child from the home if the hoarding is so bad it is endangering the child. A housing practitioner should be aware that if the child's safety is at immediate risk as a result of the hoarding (or otherwise) an application can be made to apply for an Emergency Protection Order.

An EPO is made by the court and grants authority to remove a child and places them under the protection of the applicant:

    a.   The local authority in whose area a child is found in circumstances that require emergency action (the first authority) is responsible for taking emergency action;

    b.   If the child is looked-after by, or the subject of a child protection plan in another authority, the first authority must consult the authority responsible for the child.

An EPO aims to ensure that effective action can be taken to protect children, within a framework of proper safeguards. This is why multi-agency working is crucial.

The proceedings are dealt with in Part 5 of the Children Act 1989 and are not classed as family proceedings. The court must either make or refuse to make the order. It cannot make any other kind of order unless there is an application for a child assessment order. The court must be satisfied that there are grounds for making an EPO and that such an order should be made (s.43(4)) Children Act 1989. The court must be satisfied that there is reasonable cause to believe that the child is likely to suffer significant harm if he or she:

a. Is not removed to accommodation provided by the application; or
b. Does not remain in the place when the child is then being accommodated.

It is no uncommon in hoarding cases, an EPO may also be made if enquiries are being frustrated by the unreasonable refusal of access to the child. This might be due to the hoarder feeling embarrassed about letting people into their home or fearing interference with their belongings above the needs of the child affected by their belongings and behaviour.

An EPO is for a maximum of 8 days but may be extended to 15 days. It is gives the local authority the right to remove a child to accommodation provided by or on behalf of the applicant whilst also conferring upon it limited parental responsibility for the child.

The court can attach an exclusion requirement to an EPO which can exclude the relevant person from the home, and from a designated area around the home. A power of arrest can be included.

Police Powers

Police can remove a child in an emergency but should be used only in exceptional circumstances where there is insufficient time to seek an EPO or for reasons relating to the immediate safety of the child. When a police officer has exercised this power, the child is held to be in police protection. No child may be kept in police protection for more than 72 hours. Thereafter, the case is passed to a designated office that completes an inquiry and take steps to secure accommodation provided by the local authority pursuant to sections 46(3).

Section 11 Children Act 2004 Duties

Housing and homelessness services in local authorities and others such as environmental health organisations are subject to the section 11 duties.

Practitioners working in these services may become aware of conditions that could have or are having an adverse impact on children before any-one else.

Under Part 1 of the Housing Act 2004, authorities must take account of the impact of health and safety hazards in housing when deciding on the action to be taken by landlords to improve conditions. Housing authorities also have an important role to play in safeguarding vulnerable young people.

Pursuant to covered by section 11(2) of the Children Act 2004. This requires each person or body to whom the section applies (which includes a local housing authority) to make arrangements for ensuring that:

> *"(a) their functions are discharged having regard to the need to safe-guard and promote the welfare of children; and*
> *(b) any services provided by another person pursuant to arrangements made by the person or body in the discharge of their functions are provided having regard to that need."*

Section 11 does not define 'welfare', but section 10 provides a statutory framework for co-operation between the local authority and relevant agencies with a view to improving the 'well-being' of children in the area.

Well-being is defined as:

a. physical, mental and emotional well-being;
b. protection from harm and neglect;
c. education, training and recreation;

d. the contribution made by children to society; and

e. social and economic well-being (section 10(2)).

Until 2015, it was held that section 11 has no part to play in the decision as to whether a person's actions are deliberate for the purpose of deciding whether one is intentionally homeless or not (perhaps because they have left shared accommodation that was shared with a hoarder or a partner that is a hoarder, or due to their hoarding they lost their tenancy or became the subject of a demolition order, hazard awareness notice etc). As Moses LJ pointed out in *Huzrat v Hounslow London Borough Council [2013] EWCA Civ 1865*, para 26:

> *"The statutory questions are clear; was the action or omission in question deliberate? The answer to that question cannot differ [according to] whether the local authority takes into account the duty under section 11 of the Children's [sic] Act or not."*

The decision maker should identify the principal needs of the children, both individually and collectively, and have regard to the need to safeguard and promote them when making the decision.

Section 11 does not require that the children's welfare should be the paramount consideration but does encourage partnerships between agencies and creates more accountability by:

a. placing a duty on local authorities to appoint children's services members who are ultimately accountable for the delivery of services;

b. placing a duty on local authorities and their partners to co-operate in safeguarding and promoting the wellbeing of children and young people.

Where Convention Rights under the Human Rights Act 1998 are engaged, they have to be interpreted and applied consistently with international human right standards, including the UNCRC: see *ZH (Tanzania) v Secretary of State for the Home Department [2011] UKSC 4, [2011] 2 AC 166.*

As Pitchford LJ put it, in *R (Castle) v Metropolitan Police Commissioner [2011] EWHC 2317 (Admin), [2014] 1 All ER 953*, para 51:

> *"The chief officer's statutory obligation is not confined to training and dissemination of information. It is to ensure that decisions affecting children have regard to the need to safeguard them and to promote their welfare."*

However, he went to point out that:

> *"This does not mean that the duties and functions of the police have been re-defined by section 11 ... the guidance accurately states the obligation of chief officers of police 'to carry out their existing functions in a way which takes into account the need to safeguard and promote the welfare of children'."*

CHAPTER FOUR
ANIMAL HOARDING

This chapter identifies different types of animal hoarding and the Animal Welfare Act 2006

What to look for

To hoard animals is to:

   a.   Denial of the inability to provide the care required;
      i.   Deny the impact of any failure to provide has on the animals;
      ii.   Despite this failure there is nevertheless a persistence to keep accumulating animals.
   b.   Have more than what is objectively a reasonable number of companion animals;
   c.   Failing to provide the minimum care including appropriate shelter, health care, human contact (how often and with who).

The DSM-5 definition of hoarding specifically addresses animal hoarding and uses criteria set out in the Hoarding of Animals Consortium ('HARC'). The DSM-5 notes that those who hoard animals tend to hoard objects too.

There are different forms of animal hoarding and the categories identified go beyond the basic DSM-5 definition[16].

---

[16] Frost, R. O., Patronek, G., Arluke, A., & Steketee, G. (2015). The Hoarding of Animals: An Update. *Psychiatric Times*

Types of animal hoarding

Rescue Hoarder

These individuals tend to hoard large numbers of animals in a hope to 'save' the animals even if they are incurably ill or suffering. This is the largest and most costly problem to law enforcement.

It can be challenging to deal with such individuals because they consider themselves as having a mission to save the animals. They consider themselves being the best qualified to tend to the animal's needs. They do not realise or appreciate that their retention of the animal/s causes greater harm than if they had the animal euthanised.

As a result of the seemingly positive aim and/or purpose the individual has in mind, they lack an insight into the harm that blinds them from being able to cooperate with authorities that intervene on behalf of animals as well as or in addition to the hoarder themselves.

The difficulty those in enforcement have is that such individuals are hard to detect and they often slip under the radar, not least because they refuse to take the animals to the veterinary surgery for fear that a veterinary surgeon would not be acting in the best interests of the animal itself.

Due to their belief system, there is an element of recidivism. It is often the case that the individual views their own self as being in existence merely to look after rescued animals. This means that animals can provide an ideal resource for building a strong, idealized, but ultimately erroneous self-image[17].

Exploiter Hoarding

This type of animal hoarder is motivated by financial gain from soliciting funds not then used for the care of the animals. When dealing with these individuals practitioners tend to find that they lack the ability to empathise, so they do not care about what harm comes to the animals.

---

[17] Brown, S. E. (2011). Theoretical concepts from self-psychology applied to animal hoarding. *Society & Animals, 19*, 175–193

Whilst such individuals seem competent and in control, they tend to have severe personality disorders coinciding with manipulative and narcissistic tendencies. Having animals is not just about using them to make money but they are also a way in which the individuals can exert control over something in their life[18]. The absence of emotional attachment to their animals suggests that these types of individuals are beyond the diagnostic criteria for hoarding.

However, given the lack of empathy, they are more likely to be prosecuted because their sense of oneself is more egocentric than other types of hoarding.

<u>Caregiver</u>

Middling the spectrum is the overwhelmed caregiver. It is not that money comes first, or indeed themselves, but they minimise rather than deny that there is an animal care problem. There is some recognition of their finances being the cause of their neglect of the animals. They consider it beyond their remit to remedy the animals' ill health.

The overwhelmed caregiver is strongly attached to their animals but that attachment is so strong, that ultimately, when they are no longer able to financially care for the animals, such individuals instead bury their head in the sand rather than tackle it head on by securing better funds or selling or gifting the animal to a charity, individual or organisation.

These individuals are more likely to cooperate precisely because they care about the health and wellbeing of the animal. Prosecuting these types of individuals is counterproductive. They do not necessarily show a significant, if any, impairment in social or other areas of functioning. This often means that such individuals fall outside the DSM-5 criteria. Rather than prosecuting these individuals, practitioners are encouraged to consider other legal remedies and powers such as but not limited to injunctions.

---

[18] Patronek, G. J., & Nathanson, J. N. (2009). A theoretical perspective to inform assessment and treatment strategies for
animal hoarders. *Clinical Psychology Review, 29*(3), 274–281

<u>Addiction and Childhood</u>

Excuses for hoarding with animals tend to be more commonplace, and potentially more believable, such as being socially isolated.

Addiction, however, has been connected to animal hoarding[19]:

a. Preoccupation with animals;
b. Denial of problems causing them to hoard and/or as a result of the hoarding;
c. Socially isolated;
d. Neglect of one's surroundings;
e. Impulse control.

Addictions can be reviewed as stemming from attachment problems found in animal hoarding, because of the traits one typically displays when hoarding animals[20].

Animal hoarding is usually accompanied by a history of disordered or inadequate attachments to people. Research by the HARC[21]in 2002 suggested that hoarders grew up with inconsistent parenting and animals may have been a key feature in their life. Frequent relocations, parental separation and isolation are just some of the underlying features.

Nathanson and Patronek (2011)[22] and Steketee et al. (2011)[23] have suggested that to understand the problem the focus should be on the thoughts and actions of hoarders. From this perspective, animal hoarders

---

[19] Lockwood, R. (1994). The psychology of animal collectors. *American Animal Hospital Association Trends Magazine*, 9, 18–21

[20] Flores, P. J. (2004). *Addiction as an attachment disorder*. Lantham, Maryland: Jason Aronson

[21] Hoarding of Animals Research Consortium (HARC) (2002). Health implications of animal hoarding. *Health and Social Work*

[22] Nathanson, J., & Patronek, G. (2011). Animal hoarding: How the semblance of a benevolent mission becomes actualized as egoism and cruelty. In B. Oakley, A. Knafo, G. Madhavan, & D. Wilson (Eds.), *Pathological Alltruism* (pp. 107–115). New York, NY: Oxford University Press.

[23] Steketee, G., Gibson, A., Frost, R. O., Alabiso, J. Arluke, A., & Patronek, G. (2011). Characteristics and antecedents of people who hoard animals: An exploratory comparative interview study. *Review of General Psychology, 15*(2), 114

often manifest a personality disorder such as mistrust leading to unstable and intense interpersonal relationships. This often involves feelings of emptiness and difficulty with anger. Those having these traits often come from families where they had a history of unresolved grief or emotional or physical abuse[24].

Animal hoarding may even be a way in which a hoarder finds something it can connect to which is conflict-free and is considered by the hoarder to be 'safe'. The the neglect experienced as a child may manifest itself in how the animal treated. The animal is treated in a similar way, often left abandoned.

What makes animal hoarding unique is that there is an attachment which can respond but in a way that does not question one's ability to apparently look after and care for it. This reinforces the individuals' sense of self-worth and holds themselves out as being a good person.

Legal Provisions

<u>Animal Welfare Act 2006 ('AWA 2006')</u>

Animal hoarding is on the increase with the RSPCA stating that it receives over 1,000 calls every year (see RSPCA: Cat Smart pilot project (Quarter 4 report June – August 2018)).

Section 9 of the Animal Welfare Act 2006 ('AWA 2006') imposes a duty of care requiring people to take reasonable steps to meet the welfare needs of their animals to the extent required by good practice. This includes an animal's need:

a. For a suitable environment;
b. For a suitable diet;
c. To be able to exhibit normal behaviour patterns;
d. To be protected from pain, suffering, injury and disease;

---

[24]Cassidy, J., & Mohr, J. J. (2001). Unsolvable fear, trauma, and psychopathology. *Clinical Psychology: Science and Practice, 8*, 275–298

   e.   To be housed with, or apart from, other animals.

It is likely that a hoarding environment will prevent one or more of these needs from being met and the animal concerned may be mistreated or neglected.

As an initial step, authorities should attempt to educate the property owner to prevent any further mistreatment. However, where this has not worked or the relevant individual has chosen not to engage with the authority, then an inspector is able to issue an improvement notice requiring the relevant individual to take steps to comply with section 9 and setting out the period in which this action must be taken (section 10). An inspector is defined as a person appointed by the appropriate national authority or a local authority. This could be, for example, an RSPCA inspector or a member of the environmental health team at the relevant local authority (section 51).

Following any non-compliance, a local authority (as well as the police) may prosecute the individual concerned (section 30). Potential sanctions include a fine of up to £20,000, up to 51 weeks imprisonment, and a prohibition from owning or dealing with animals in the future (although such a ban is difficult to enforce).

The key issue here for local authorities is ensuring the welfare of any animals at the property, which may involve removal. Authorities should work in partnership with bodies such as the RSPCA to ensure that the individual concerned is educated to safely look after, and to only keep a reasonable number of, animals.

CHAPTER FIVE

HOARDING AND HOW ONE CAN USE THE ENVIRONMENTAL HEALTH ACT 1990, HOUSING ACT 2004 AND RELATED STATUTORY PROVISIONS

This chapter looks at the various options for securing clearance or otherwise of a property

Housing Act 2004 ('HA 2004')

Part 3 of the Environmental Protection Act 1990 ('EPA 1990') gives local authorities powers to require the abatement of several issues, including where the physical state of premises amounts to a statutory nuisance (section 79).

Much of this legislation can be used by tenants, occupiers and/or their neighbours to force work/s to be done to improve the condition of the property. Part 3 is concerned with tackling the effects of bad housing. This is particularly useful if the property is unhealthy or otherwise in poor condition but there is no civil remedy because there is no breach of contract or any other civil 'wrong.' There is no restriction on who can raise a complaint about conditions with the local authority and request an inspection under the Housing Act 2004 (section 3(3)(a), ('HA 2004').

Procedure

If the local housing authority considers that it would be appropriate to inspect the property under Part 1 of the HA 2004, then it must arrange for an inspection to be carried out pursuant to section 4(2). The local housing authority should ensure that their contact details are publicly available and accessible.

The local housing authority should act within a reasonable period of time because a failure to do so may lead to an 'official complaint' to be lodged by a justice of the peace for the area pursuant to section 4. This is not the same as the local housing authority's complaint procedure. Should the local housing authority receive an official complaint it is bound to consider the report from the inspecting officer if the inspecting officer is of the view that a hazard exists (section 4(6)) and inspect the property pursuant to section 4(2). Whilst there is no statutory timetable within which the local housing authority must respond to official complaints it should attend to the same and inspect the property as soon as possible (section 4(6) (7)). Thereafter, any delay will leave judicial review open to the applicant where a mandatory order may be obtained to require the local housing authority to act.

It is sometimes the case that the local housing authority has tried to access the property but has been prevented from doing so. The local housing authority may, in that event, consider applying for an injunction or exercise its powers of entry pursuant to section 239(3) of the HA 2004. Notice of at least 24 hours should be given if powers of entry are to be exercised but if there is reasonable concern that there is a certain offence being committed or that emergency remedial action is required, then immediate access may be obtained under section 239(3) without giving prior notice, see subsections 5 and 6. Any hesitation to not use legal powers available to it would be frowned upon in the Administrative Division of the High Court in the event that an application for judicial review is made.

Assessment

The local housing authority Environmental Health Officer ('EHO') is looking to see if the property is 'unfit for human habitation' or 'in substantial repair'.

A 'hazard' means any risk to the health and safety of an actual or potential occupier of a dwelling which arises from a deficiency in the dwelling or in any building or land in the vicinity (section 2(1)). Harm can include temporary harm and health includes mental health (sections 2(4) and (5)).

Serious hazards are categorised as Category 1. Category 2 hazards are less serious. If there is a Category 1 hazard the local housing authority is under an obligation to take action. Category 2 hazards do not demand the local housing authority to take any action but it has the statutory power to do so.

The assessment itself is carried out by the local housing authority officials and regard must be given to the Operating Guidance and the Enforcement Guidance:

a. Assess the likelihood of a person suffering harm as a result of any hazard;
b. Assess probable consequences of the hazard;
c. Give a numerical score using prescribed methodology (see Chapter Nine, Clutter Image Rating Scale);
d. Consider the numerical score against the banding and whether that banding falls within category 1 or 2.

There are 29 hazards set out in the HHRS Hazards Regulations 2005 in Schedule 1. These are extensive and the hazards set out include crowding and space, domestic hygiene, pests and refuse, sanitation, and other hazards. These listed herein are perhaps more likely to be seen when dealing with a case of hoarding.

Courses of Action

There are different enforcement actions available:

a. Declaring a clearance area;
b. Issuing an improvement notice;
c. Making a prohibition order;
d. Making a demolition order (possible in hoarding cases if the integrity of the building has been affected by the sheer volume of items);
e. Hazard awareness notice (also likely in hoarding cases).

If it is a category hazard, then there is also the option to take emergency remedial action or make an emergency prohibition order.

Only one course of action can be taken at any one time.

a. Declaring a clearance area

This is where the residential buildings in an area contains a category 1 hazard and non-residential buildings in the same area are dangerous. This was principally aimed at slums but can also be used to address areas of unsatisfactory housing. One may be compensated or rehoused by the local housing authority if this happens.

A clearance area is an area to be cleared of all buildings. (section 289 of the Housing Act 1985 as amended by section 47 of the HA 2004):

a. Each residential building has a category 1 hazard; or
b. Residential buildings in the area are too dangerous or are harmful to health and safety of inhabitants in the areas or;
c. Each residential building contains a category 2 hazard but is in an areas that is dangerous or harmful to the health and safety of inhabitants in the areas and the secretary of state has considered the circumstances of the case in an order;

This normally results in compulsory purchase acquisitions and the clearing of the site in readiness for renewal.

b. Improvement notice

This requires the recipient of the notice to address the hazards identified, and for such work/s to not start earlier than 28 days after service of the notice (*Odeniran v Southend-on-Sea BC [2013] EWHC 3888 (Admin), [2014] HLR 11*. Statutorily prescribed information must be included pursuant to section 13.

c. Prohibition order

This prohibits the use of the property for such categorises of use as the order describes pursuant to section 20. It must set out the hazard and action need before the order can be revoked.

d. Demolition order

The procedures for this is set out in Part 9 of the Housing Act 1985 and 'demolition order' is defined therein at section 265, as amended by section 46 of the HA 2004.

This order requires the owner to demolish the property after it has been vacated and the site cleared. This means that the property ceases to be used for human habitation.

e. Hazard awareness notice

This is a notification to the recipient of the existence of Category 1 and/or 2 hazard/s. It is a formal notice to forewarn a recipient that they might consider it wise to remedy the same.

f. Emergency Action/s

This arises where there is an 'imminent risk of serious harm' this can include entering the property to carry out emergency works pursuant to sections 40 to 42 of the HA 2004. Service of a notice of emergency remedial action is given pursuant to section 40 of the HA 2004.

Environmental Protection Act 1990 ('EPA 1990')

The provisions of Part 3 in the EPA 1990 are therefore likely to be wide enough to cover issues associated with hoarding, for example, pest infestation. A problem with fleas is deemed to be the responsibility of the tenant or leaseholder. Therefore, if a local authority's pest control service undertakes to resolve a flea infestation, the authority can recover incurred costs from the occupier, although the service can use its discretion as to whether to charge.

The EPA 1990 also gives local authorities a power of entry to determine if a statutory nuisance exists or to undertake works to prevent such a nuisance (schedule 3). This is likely to be useful in a hoarding context where the relevant individual is unwilling to engage or allow entry to inspect their property. However, in the context of a domestic property, notice should generally be given before entry is attempted.

Statutory nuisances likely to be identified in hoarding cases include:

a. Any premiss in such a state as to be prejudicial to health or a nuisance (section 79(1)(a));
b. Any accumulation or deposit which is prejudicial to health or a nuisance (section 79(1)(e)).

<u>Section 79(1)(a)</u>

Premises is defined to include all land and vessels, occupied or not. Private rented and social housing are covered. In *Birmingham CC v Oakley [2000] UKHL 59; [2001] 33 HLR 283*, the courts have held that the Act is concerned with the condition of the property, not the way it is used. This means that any enforcement taken under this Act will not necessarily prevent the problem arising again if the root cause, hoarding, is not addressed. It is a sticking plaster and management of consequences only.

Premises includes individuals flats as well as entire blocks of flats. It includes an open site without permanent buildings such as travellers' sites. The statutory nuisance arises if the premises as a whole is in such as state as to be prejudicial to health or is a nuisance. The aim, therefore, is restricted to public health matters.

To be prejudicial to health the statutory nuisance arises where the property (premises) is in such a state, whether due to hoarding, disrepair, a latent defect or otherwise, as to be prejudicial to health. This means to be 'injurious to likely to cause injury, to health' (section 79(7)) This is an objective test and includes potential, as well as actual ill health. This includes those who are already ill but their condition is likely to deteriorate further as a result of the state and condition of the property, see *Malton Bourgh Health Board v Malton Farmers Manure Co (1879) 4 Ex D 302*. It not confined to physical health but includes mental health as well.

To be a nuisance it must be a public nuisance or private nuisance at common law, see *National Coal Board v Neath BC [1976] 2 All ER 478, DC* that explains the distinction:

a. Public: act or omission that adversely affects the comfort and quality of the public or class of people;
b. Private: substantial interference with the use and enjoyment of neighbouring property. The damage suffered need not be continuing, see *Wandsworth London Borough Council v Railtrack plc [2002] QB 756, [2002] 2 WLR 512, CA.*

Most importantly, the nuisance must relate to matters of public health, *Coventry CC v Cartwright [1975] 1 WLR 845; [1975] 2 All ER 99, DC.* The failure to act does not mean that the defendant must carry out extensive investigations to discover the harm or potential harm. The duty is owed only if there is foreseeability and proximity of harm, as well as whether the duty itself is fair, just and reasonable considering the individual concerned such as whether they are labouring under a disability or disorder such as hoarding.

Schedule 3, paragraph 2 of the EPA 1990 permits an EHO to enter and inspect a property which may in such a state as to be a statutory nuisance. Steps to be taken must be those that are regarded as reasonably practicable.

A local housing authority may find that one may approach it to request what is called environmental information pursuant to the Environmental Information Regulation 2004 (SI No 3391) regulation 2. There are two exceptions at regulation 12:

a. Standalone exceptions;
b. Adverse effect exceptions.

Nevertheless, the statutory presumption is in favour of disclosure pursuant to regulation 12(2).

Enforcement

Informal Notice

If the EHO is satisfied that there is a statutory nuisance (or it likely to arise), then the local housing authority is bound to take action, see *Cocker v Cardwell (1869) LR 5 QB 15.*

Practitioners may choose to serve an informal notice first and it is noticeable that some local authorities have their own enforcement protocols. If an informal notice is sent it is suggested that there notice set out what the consequences could be if the nuisance is not abated and/or removed and/or the cause is not resolved With a hoarder, however this is unlikely to be acted upon because they do not necessarily see that they have a problem giving rise toa statutory nuisance in the first place.

A more formal approach would be to serve a abatement notice pursuant to section 80(1) of the EPA 1990. This requires the abatement of the nuisance and any works necessary for that purpose within a specified timeframe. For the avoidance of doubt, this is not a preliminary step to court proceedings. The notice must be clear and enable the recipient to understand what is required. The penal sanctions must also be clearly set out in the event if non-compliance. In hoarding cases, this is particularly helpful. If certain work/s are suggested then these must be capable of being remedied, see *Network Housing Association Ltd v Westminster CC [1994] Times, 14 April, CA*, even though the local housing authority has a choice about what notice to serve if any, see *Budd v Colchester Borough Council [1999] Env LR 739, CA*.

Abatement Notice

The abatement notice must be served on the person responsible for the nuisance (section 80(2)(a), as inserted by section 86 of the Clean Neighbourhoods and Environment Act 2005). Pursuant to section 79(7) this is the person to whose act, default or suffer the nuisance is attributable

If the hoarding has caused structural defects, then the notice must be served on the owner (section 80(2)(b)). If the property is being used to hoard items and the hoarder cannot themselves be located, and the person upon whom to serve the notice, then the local authority must serve the notice on the occupier or owner (depending on the nature of the hoarder's occupation (tenant or owner)), section 80(2)(c),

If there is more than one person responsible, which may be the case of a couple that are hoarders, then the notice may be served on each person whether or not their conduct or default alone would amount to a nuisance, section 81(1).

Once served with such a notice, one has the right to appeal to the magistrates' court within 21 days of the date of service of the notice., section 80(3). This is by way of a complaint. Pursuant to schedule 3 paragraph 1(2).

The basis on which one may appeal is set out in the Statutory Nuisance (Appeals) Regulations 1995 SI No 2644 as amended by SI No 771 (2006). Examples include:

a. Equality Act 2010 – failure to consider that the individual served is labouring under a mental disability that is causing them to hoard;
b. Not served on the correct party;
c. Errors in the notice;
d. Mental Capacity Act 2005 – the individual/s served lacks the capacity to understand what has been served and/or but for their lacking of capacity, would not hoard and cause the subsequent nuisance (private or public).

If the notice is not appeal or is not complied with, then the person served is guilty of an offence unless there is a reasonable excuse. The local housing authority does not have to prosecute for a failure to comply with such a notice, but the option is there. If the individual concerned is suspected to be a hoarder, it is suggested that action dealing with the hoarding behaviour itself be considered and carried out first such as a Care Act assessment, Mental Capacity assessment etc. There is otherwise a real danger of breaching sections 19 and/or 15 of the Equality Act 2010 (indirect and direct discrimination) and/or Article 8 of the ECHR. Furthermore, such actions, if not taken without due regard for the fact that one may be labouring under a disability or impaired cognitive function by reason of their hoarding, could result in a judicial review claim whereby a declaration of a breach of one's human rights, and specifically that of disability discrimination, may be sought.

If the offence of a failure to comply is proven, then the person liable to a fine up to level 5 on the standard scale and a further fine of one-tenth the level 5 scale for each day after conviction of non-compliance, section 80(5). For the avoidance of doubt, level 5 is an unlimited fine, as amended by section 85 of the Legal Aid, Sentencing and Punishment of Offenders Act ('LASPO') 2012.

An authority can also apply for a High Court injunction where an abatement notice would by itself be inadequate (section 81).

Where an abatement notice is not complied with, a local authority can abate the nuisance itself by carrying out the necessary works and recharging reasonable expenses to the person responsible (section 81(4)). The local authority may choose to serve a notice stating its intention to the do the remedial work/s should the recipient of the abatement notice fail to do so. A period of nine days must be given before the local authority can step in and start doing the works. A counter-notice may be served within 7 days of receipt by recipient of the notice from the local authority. The local authority cannot the act unless the owner/occupier fails to start remedial work/s within a reasonable period of time or, having started the remedial works, progress has been slow.

Injunction

If the local housing authority would rather have access to other remedies such an injunction or wider means of enforcement, then proceedings can be brought in the High Court. If the local housing authority is of the view that the criminal proceedings are inadequate, then the power to reach that opinion must be properly delegated. It can be reached by a committee sub-committee or officer of the council, but not be made by a single member (*R v Secretary of State for the Environment, ex p London Borough of Hillingdon [1986] 1 WLR 192*. The decision ought not be made before a claim is issued or soon afterwards. Delegation, on the other hand, cannot be done retrospectively (see *Bowyer, Philpott and Payne Ltd v Mather [1919] 1 KB 419*).

Should an injunction be sought such a remedy cannot be obtained under section 81(5) unless an abatement notice has first been served under section 80(1).

Criminal proceedings cannot be considered inadequate merely because they are not as convenient, see *Vale of White Horse District Council v Allen & Partners [1997] Env LR 212.* In *City of Bradford Metropolitan Council v Brown and others [1987] 19 HLR 16,* the Court of Appeal considered the preceding legislation containing the same power as under section 81(5) of the EPA 1990. It cautioned that even though the court has jurisdiction to grant an injunction to restrain a breach of the criminal law, it will normally only do so where there has been a complete disregard for the statutory prohibition. Practitioners ought to tread carefully and exercise reluctance when dealing with hoarders because they probably do not appreciate the danger/s of what they are doing and/or the nuisance they are causing, even if this is explained to them. A court is also likely to be reluctant to grant an injunction which makes a defendant liable to a penalty which is much greater than the penalty imposed for the offence.

When considering such an application for injunction, therefore the local housing authority should carefully consider the impact it could have on one's human rights. A failure to do so could be a bar to the granting of the injunction. The EHCR will play a part in the discretion to be exercised by the judge as to whether and in what terms to grant an injunctive remedy.

Plainly, the Public Sector Equality Duty ('PSED') pursuant to section 149 will apply (see further below).

Section 149(1) sets out the PSED which requires that a public authority:

> "*must, in the exercise of its functions, have due regard to the need to: (a) eliminate discrimination, harassment, victimisation and any other conduct that is prohibited by or under this Act; (b) advance equality of opportunity between persons who share a relevant protected characteristic and persons who do not share it.*"

Section 149(3) provides that:

> "*having due regard to the need to advance equality of opportunity between persons who share a relevant protected characteristic and persons who do not share it involves having due regard, in particular, to the need to: (a) remove or minimise disadvantages suffered by*

> *persons who share a relevant protected characteristic that are con-*
> *nected to that characteristic [and] (b) take steps to meet the needs of*
> *persons who share a relevant protected characteristic that are different*
> *from the needs of persons who do not share it.....".*

Section 149(4) provides that

> *"the steps involved in meeting the needs of disabled persons that are*
> *different from the needs of persons who are not disabled include, in*
> *particular, steps to take account of disabled persons' disabilities."*

Further, section 149(6) recognises that

> *"compliance with the duties in this section may involve treating some*
> *persons more favourably than others; but that is not to be taken as*
> *permitting conduct that would otherwise be prohibited by or under*
> *this Act".*

It is likely to be rare that a person will be aggrieved with a local housing authority for failing to inspect a property rather than its failure to investigate his or her particular complaint of a statutory nuisance. If there is evidence of the absence of a scheme of inspection, on the other hand, this is likely to support the view that the local housing authority has not properly discharged the PSED.

A local housing authority is unlikely to be able to plead successfully that lack of resources is the reason for its failure to discharge the PSED properly. It should take into account the question of finances in deciding what method of inspection it should employ (and enforcement), see *R v Gloucestershire County Council, ex p Barry [1997] AC 584*. If the result of considering the financial consequences is to employ a method of action or enforcement that is not as effective than if the local housing authority spent greater money on the matter, then community groups and individuals could call to question the methodology and decision making adopted. Assessing how it will carry out its duty and allocate resources for inspection of an area or property and its connection to the PSED is arguable following *R (Harris) v Haringey LBC [2010] EWCA Civ 703*.

When considering an injunction, the local authority is no longer necessarily having to consider the principles of *Shelfer v City of London Electric Lighting Co [1895] 1 Ch 287*:

a. If the injury to the applicant's legal right is small;
b. Is it one which is capable of being estimate in money;
c. Is it one which can be compensated by money;
d. Is the injunction sought oppressive.

The case of *Coventry and others v Lawrence and Others [2014] UKSC 13* confirmed that a more flexible approach than the *Shelfer* test can be considered.

Building Act 1984

Section 76 – 'dangerous structure' and 'defective building'

Sometimes the enforcement procedures aforesaid is not sufficiently quick or insufficient within themselves to address what is a 'prejudice to health'. For urgent cases there are emergency procedures set out in section 76 of the Building Act 1984 that can be considered.

This enables the local housing authority to deal with dangerous buildings that have may have become dangerous due to the compulsive hoarding causing joists and flooring to give way and/or cause the property to subside.

The term 'dangerous structure' means any building, part of a building o other structure where it poses a serious danger to the public.

A 'defective building' does not pose a serious danger but will have an impact on the visual amenity of an area, and the welfare of the public therein.

Section 77 – procedure

Pursuant to section 77, the local authority may apply to the magistrates' court if the building is dangerous. The court may:

  a. Where the danger arises from the condition of the building or structure – make an order requiring the owner to:
    i. Execute such work/s as may be necessary to obviate the danger; or
    ii. Demolish the building or structure, or any dangerous part of it, and remove any rubbish resulting from the demolition.
  b. Where the danger arises from overloading (as is the case in hoarding), the local authority can request an order restricting its use until the court withdraws or modifies the restriction.

Should one not comply upon service of the order, then the local authority may:

  a. Execute the order, and
  b. Recover the expenses reasonably incurred by it in doing so form the person at fault.

Criminally, the person may also be liable to pay a fine not exceeding level 1 on the standard scale.

<u>Section 78 – emergency measures</u>

Pursuant to section 78, there are emergency measures available where:

  a. If the building or part of a building or structure is in such a state or is used to carry such loads as to be dangerous; and
  b. Immediate action should be taken to remove the danger, then the local authority may take necessary steps.

The local authority can recover the costs reasonably incurred pursuant to sections 78(3)-(6). The court has the discretion to:

  a. Not award expenses if the local authority could have used powers under section 77 instead;
  b. Decide whether some of the expenses should be paid by another person
  c. Make an order proportionate to the court.

Owners may claim compensation for any damage incurred as a result of the local authority's action/s if the owner or occupier can show there has been no default of any obligations under the Building Act 1984.

Prevention of Damage by Pests Act 1949 ('PDPA 1949)

Section 4 of the Prevention of Damage by Pests Act 1949 ('PDPA 1949') gives local authorities the power to require an owner or occupier of a property to act to prevent or treat an infestation of rats or mice. The owner or occupier of the property should be served with a notice setting out reasonable steps to destroy the rats or mice within a reasonable period. Steps could include removing materials from land or premises, carrying out structural work or carrying out pest control treatment.

Where there is a failure to carry out the steps specified, the relevant local authority may carry these out and recover the costs from the notice recipient (section 5).

It should be noted that there is no specific power of entry under section 5 of the PDPA 1949. Therefore, a local authority will not be able to carry out the necessary works if they are denied access, which could be likely in a hoarding case where the individual concerned does not want to engage with the local authority or treat any infestation. Where the owner of the land is not the occupier, separate notices may be served on both. If the occupier of the property prevents the owner carrying out the required works, the court may order the occupier to permit the work to be carried out.

This power is generally exercised by local authorities in relation to the clearing of gardens and external spaces rather than for internal clearance (where the Public Health Act 1936 powers tend to be used, see Housing Act 2004 (HHSRS)).

Clean Neighbourhoods and Environment Act 2005 ('the 2005 Act')

This provides local authorities with powers to tackle poor environmental quality and anti-social behaviour, including amendments to the Refuse

Disposal (Amenity) Act 1978. It includes sections on nuisance and abandoned vehicles, litter, graffiti, waste, noise and dogs.

Refuse Disposal (Amenity) Act 1978

This piece of legislation is likely to be relied on by local authorities where the hoarding is visible and affecting the amenity of an area, however, it does require the relevant owner to have abandoned the hoarded item/s, which in many cases would be unlikely given the nature of hoarding.

Abandoned Vehicles

This Act is generally used in cases of abandoned vehicle/s, which may be the chosen item of a hoarder to accumulate. Section 2 places a duty on local authorities to remove motor vehicles abandoned on land in the open air and can recover its costs from either the owner or the person who abandoned it.

Section 2A (as inserted by the Clean Neighbourhoods and Environment Act 2005) gives an authorised officer the power to issue a fixed penalty notice in respect of an offence of abandoning a vehicle. Section 2B enables an authorised officer to require the name and address of the person to whom he proposes to issue a fixed penalty notice and section 2C enables local authorities to use the receipts from these penalties for the purposes of their functions under the 1978 Act and sections 99 to 102 of the Road Traffic Regulation Act 1984.

No notice is required to be given by the local authority where a vehicle is abandoned on a road. Once the authority is satisfied the vehicle has been abandoned it can be removed immediately. Section 11 of the 2005 Act amends section 3 of the 1978 Act. Section 11(2) removes the requirement to serve a notice on the occupier of land where the vehicle is on a 'road'. The 2005 Act enables local authorities to immediately remove any vehicle in such a condition that it thinks it has been abandoned. The fixed penalty notice amount is £200.

Abandoned vehicles should not be confused with untaxed vehicles. Untaxed vehicles are not classed as abandoned. It is the responsibility, in that event, for the DVLA to remove, If the vehicle/s is causing an obstruction then it can be removed and dealt with by the police pursuant to relevant traffic regulations and police powers. Untaxed vehicles on private land can be removed if it is not SORN and/or is not on the property/land with permission. This includes removal from secure car parks and/or public car parks.

<u>Nuisance parking</u>

These offences are aimed at businesses that use the public road as a 'showroom' and people who use the road as a 'workshop'. The latter is more likely with hoarders.

Of most relevance is section 4 of the 2005 Act whereby it is an offence to carry out 'restricted works' to vehicles on a road. 'Restricted Works' covers repair, maintenance, servicing, improving or the dismantling of a motor vehicle or any part or accessory. The maximum fine is level 4 on the standard scale on summary conviction. The power to issue a fixed penalty notice is found at section 6 and the amount is £100.

Public Health Act 1961

Section 34 of the Public Health Act 1961 empowers a local authority to remove accumulations of rubbish that are seriously detrimental to the amenity of a neighbourhood, such as the garden of a hoarder's property. 'Rubbish' includes rubble, wastepaper, crockery, metal and any other kind of refuse (including organic matter).

A notice should be served on the relevant owner and occupier of the land at least 28 days before any action is taken outlining the proposed steps to be taken and reliance on section 34. The notice recipient and any other person with an interest in the land may, within 28 days of being served the notice, either:

a.   Serve a counter notice stating that they will take those steps;

b.   Appeal to the magistrates' court on the grounds that the local authority was not justified in taking action or the steps proposed were unreasonable.

There is also a power under section 36 of the Public Health Act 1961 to require the vacation of the affected premises while fumigation is being undertaken to destroy any vermin. This power could be used by a local authority in conjunction with section 83 of the Public Health Act 1936. Where this is required by a local authority, it must provide alternative shelter or accommodation free of charge for the relevant individual until the fumigation is complete.

Public Health Act 1936

There are several provisions in the Public Health Act 1936 ('PHA 1936') which may be appropriate in a hoarding case.

Pursuant to section 79, a local authority has the power to require removal of noxious matter by occupiers of premises in an urban district if it appears to the proper officer of the authority that the accumulation of such matter ought to be removed. Under this section, a local authority may recover the expenses of any action taken from the relevant owner or occupier in default. This provision is not generally relied on by authorities as more recent legislation exists which is more appropriate.

Section 83 requires the cleansing of any premises which are in a *"filthy or unwholesome condition as to be prejudicial to health or are verminous"*. This provision has been held to include the hoarding of excrement and infestation of premises by rats, mice and insects.

Under this provision, a notice should be served on the owner or occupier of the premises requiring certain steps to be taken within a stated period (generally a minimum of 21 days) to remedy their condition (this may require the removal of wall coverings or the destruction or removal of any vermin). A failure to comply with a notice under section 83 will allow a local authority to undertake the works itself and to recover the costs from the owner. There is no appeal against the issue of such a notice.

Section 84 gives local authorities a power to cleanse, purify, disinfect or destroy any filthy or verminous articles found in a property at their own expense.

CHAPTER SIX

HOARDING AND HOW AND WHEN TO USE INJUNCTIONS AND ANTI-SOCIAL BEHAVIOUR ACT 2014

This chapter considers the application of the Anti-Social Behaviour Act 2014 and the way proceedings can be conducted if an Anti-Social Behaviour Injunction ('ASBI') is sought. There is also consideration of the rules and sentencing when one is being committed for breach

Section 2

Section 2(1)(c) of the Anti-Social Behaviour Act 2014 ('2014 Act') concerns 'housing related nuisance' so that a direct or indirect interference with housing management functions of a provider or local authority.

To determine if an injunction is appropriate the landlord (private, housing association or local authority) must first consider the occupier's mental capacity.

Purpose

An injunction would compel one to do or not do specific activities. An injunction may be obtained under section 1. This can include:

a. Compelling one to permit contractors to attend the property (and ask for possession/s to be moved to facilitate the work(s));
b. Compelling one to clear the property and/or make it more fire safe.

The applicant must show that on a balance of probabilities, the hoarder is engaged or threatens to engage in anti-social behaviour, and that it is just and convenient to grant the injunction for the purpose of preventing an engagement in such behaviour. The injunction is available in the county court for adults and in the youth court (sitting in its civil capacity) for under 18s and rests on the civil standard of proof. There is no minimum or maximum term for an injunction for adults.

An injunction, however, does not deal with the underlying cause/s for the hoarding. However, an injunction could be used to encourage the tenant to address the underlying causes of their behaviour. They can be encouraged to cooperate with support services which may in turn address underlying issues. The greater the requirements that are 'positive' the more likely they are to be successful and decrease the likelihood of the hoarder breaching the injunction. Either way, the applicant must show that they can enforce the injunction and monitor the condition/s thereto.

'Anti-social behaviour' is defined as:

a.   conduct that has caused, or is likely to cause, harassment, alarm or distress to any person (*Birmingham City Council v Pardoe [2016] EWHC 3119*);

b.   conduct capable of causing nuisance or annoyance to a person in relation to that person's occupation of residential premises (applies only where the injunction under section 1 is applied for by a housing association, a local housing authority, or a chief officer of police);

c.   conduct capable of causing housing-related nuisance or annoyance to any person.

In *Leeds City Council v Persons Unknown [2015] QBD*, HHJ Saffman held that local authorities should not seek to use powers under section 222 Local Government Act to obtain injunctions using the common law to restrain or prevent persistent behaviour that could be regarded as anti-social; rather they should use the statutory remedies set out in the 2014 Act;

An order can be made on notice, or without notice, and can contain prohibitions or requirements. A power of arrest can be attached to all, or part, of the order if the court thinks that:

a. the anti-social behaviour in which the tenant/s has engaged or threatens to engage in consists of or includes the use or threatened use of violence against other persons, or

b. there is a significant risk of harm to other persons from the tenant/s.

Given the nature of hoarding, it is not desirable nor likely for a power of arrest to be attached to the order.

The Home Office published statutory guidance in July 2014, Anti-social Behaviour, Crime and Policing Act 2014: Anti-social behaviour powers Statutory guidance for frontline professionals ('the guidance'). It was updated in December 2017 and August 2019. The guidance has emphasised the importance of ensuring that the powers are used appropriately to provide a proportionate response to the specific behaviour that is causing harm or nuisance, without impacting adversely on behaviour that is neither unlawful nor anti-social. This is why the multi-agency approach at Chapter 2 is important. Other interventions relevant to hoarding include:

a. warning (verbal or written);
b. community resolution;
c. referral to social services;
d. liaising with the NHS Liaison and Diversion Service ('L&D')

L&D

This service identifies people with mental health, learning disability, substance misuse or other vulnerabilities when they first come into contact with the criminal justice system as suspects, defendants or offenders. It then provides assessment and assistance through diversion from the courts. Unfortunately, the civil courts do not appear linked to the services at all and concerns have been raised by the judiciary. The advantage of an L&D practitioner is that they have immediate access to medical records so they can advise of any diagnosed condition or medication. In hoarding, such L&D services, therefore, are advantageous. This means that if there is a referral the cause of the anti-social behaviour and/or nuisance and/or annoyance (the hoarding itself) is considered, identified, and potentially resolved.

The L&D service also provides outreach support. The L&D service is able to provide updated information to any court reviewing a sentence or order.

Commencing proceedings

An application is made under Part 8 of the Civil Procedure Rules ('CPR') as mandated (and modified) by Part 65.43(1).

It may be made at any county court hearing centre and must be supported by a witness statement filed with the claim form. The claim form must state the terms of the injunction applied for, see CPR 65.43(3)(a). Notice of an application should be given. The rules require service of the application notice and witness statement no less than two days before the hearing: see CPR 65.43(6)(a). However, section 6 of the 2014 Act provides that an applications for an injunction under section 1 may be made without notice. CPR Part 65.43(4)(a) requires that the witness statement must state the reasons why notice has not been given this may include worsening behaviour and/or urgency. This is unlikely to arise in hoarding since the consequences of hoarding tend to be slow burning and are often noticed before it becomes urgent only in exceptional circumstances should one be applied for without notice.

In *Birmingham City Council v Afsar and others [2019] EWHC 1560 (QB)* Mr Justice Warby discharged injunctions under the 2014 Act obtained without notice and emphasised the duties upon an applicant seeking an injunction without notice to the respondent:

> *"If the applicant does make an application for an interim injunction without giving notice: a) the evidence in support of the application must state the reasons why notice has not been given": CPR 25.3(3); b) The applicant comes under a duty to make full and frank disclosure to the Court of all matters of fact and law that are material to the application: Civil Procedure 2019 n 25.3.5. This is a broader*

obligation than the one specified in PD25A para 3.3 ("the evidence must set out ... all material facts of which the Court should be made aware"). c) The applicant (including its Counsel and solicitors) has a duty to make a note of the hearing, including but not limited to a note of the Court's judgment, and to serve this on the respondent without delay: Civil Procedure 2019, n 25.3.10.... It is worth expanding a little on some of these points, starting with the question of applications without notice. A series of authorities has emphasised how exceptional it is for the Court to grant an injunction or other order against an absent party, who has not had notice of the application and a chance to dispute it. The principle that the Court should hear both sides of the argument is an "elementary" rule of justice and "[a]s a matter of principle no order should be made in civil or family proceedings without notice to the other side unless there is very good reason for departing from the general rule that notice should be given": Moat Housing Group South Ltd v Harris [2005] EWCA Civ 287 [2006] QB 606 [63], [71-72] (a case of alleged antisocial behaviour by a tenant)."

and

"These are the principles relating to disclosure of facts. As to the law, the authorities are clear: there is a "high duty to make full, fair and accurate disclosure ... and to draw the court's attention to significant ... legal and procedural aspects of the case": Memory Corp v Sidhu (No 2) [2001] 1 WLR 1443 (CA), 1459-60. The duty is owed by the lawyers also. "It is the particular duty of the advocate to see that ... at the hearing the court's attention is drawn by him to ... the applicable law and to the formalities and procedure to be observed".

Capacity issues

A tenant/s must have capacity and must be able to understand the proceedings and the implications of any order made. The tenant/s mental impairment means that he/she is truly incapable of complying with its conditions. Such an order is incapable of protecting the public and therefore it cannot be said to be necessary to protect the public; see generally *Wookey v Wookey [1991] Fam 121.*

It is important for the court to consider capacity so that it can be confident that if there is a breach it is because one understands that they are committing a breach, and the implications of the same. When considering capacity there must be a pragmatic way of approaching it. This includes considering the consequences that would follow from the continuation of litigation without appointment of a litigation friend or Official Solicitor.

Collins J pointed out the difficulties with this course in *IS (by the Official Solicitor v (1) Director of Legal Aid Casework (2) The Lord Chancellor [2015] EWHC 1965 (Admin):*

> *"The OS has particular concerns for patients, namely persons lacking mental capacity, and children who cannot engage in litigation without a litigation friend. He is a litigation friend of last resort in the sense that he will act only where no other litigation friend can be found. He will not, save in rare cases, himself conduct litigation and needs to have external funding. There is a powerful disincentive for a litigation friend to act since he or she undertakes not only to pay the protected persons costs but any costs that the court may order to be paid by the protected person. While the litigation friend will expect to recover from the protected person such costs, that is unlikely to be realistic when the protected person lacks means and so could be financially eligible for legal aid. Equally, a litigation friend is under a duty to act always in the protected person's best interests and those may not be in accordance with the protected person's views, albeit those views must always be put to the court. Thus in many cases it would be inappropriate for a family member (for example a parent of a child) to act as a litigation friend since there may be a need for objectivity which could not be met. Further, McKenzie friends cannot be used. It follows that in many cases involving impecunious children or adults who lack capacity there will be real difficulties in finding a litigation friend prepared to act having regard in particular to liability for costs. Thus the OS may have to act if approached. He will not normally be able to act for an impecunious individual,*

unless, absent a CFA or a costs undertaking from the opposing party, there is legal aid."

Some people have mental and/or physical conditions which render them vulnerable and hamper their access to justice and some are vulnerable by reason of the subject matter of the proceedings before the court, such as ASBI and/or potential eviction. If one is vulnerable, which is more than likely in a case of hoarding then section 16 of the Anti-social Behaviour, Crime and Policing Act 2014 applies whereby special measures can be put in place to accommodate for one's vulnerability in proceedings. See also section 17 where such measures are sought because one is distressed. Special measures are not set out in the CPR but include pursuant to sections 23 to 28:

a. screening a witness from the accused;
b. allowing evidence by live link;
c. removal of court attire such as wigs;
d. pre-recorded evidence in chief;
e. pre-recorded cross examination;
f. examination through an intermediary and/or providing aids to communication;
g. allowing evidence to be given in private.

Contempt of Court

Committal Applications

Committal proceedings are dealt with under Civil Procedure Rule 81 ('CPR') and are made under Part 23 and are relied upon in the event of an ASBI being breached. The standard of proof is the criminal standard of beyond reasonable doubt. From 1 October 2020, a substantially revised CPR 81 will be in force. CPR 81.4 will state:

> *"81.4(1) Unless and to the extent that the court directs otherwise, every contempt application must be supported by written evidence given by affidavit or affirmation."*

An affidavit must comply with the requirements set out in Practice Direction 32. The Court may waive any procedure defect in the commencement or conduct of the committal application if satisfied that no injustice has been caused to the tenant/s by the defect. Committal proceedings for breach of an Injunction are civil proceedings to which the rules in CPR Part 32 (Evidence) apply.

Hearsay evidence is admissible in respect of committal proceedings and is governed by the Civil Evidence Act 1995. Although committal proceedings are categorised as criminal for the purposes of the Human Rights Act 1998, the admission of hearsay evidence on committal applications is not precluded by Article 6, see *Daltel Europe Ltd (In Liquidation) v Makki (Committal for Contempt) [2006] EWCA Civ 94; [2006] 1 W.L.R. 2704 (per* Lloyd LJ at para. 46, 56 and 59).

District judges had the jurisdiction to deal with committals in respect of breaches of injunctions under the Housing Act 1996 arising from antisocial behaviour. After the 2014 Act came into force some confusion arose as to whether district judges had the jurisdiction to make committal orders in respect of breaches of the 2014 Act. In 2018, the jurisdiction was confirmed by amendments to Practice Direction 2B and CPR 65.47(5).

CPR 65 provides a power to deal with the contempt at this hearing or within 28 days without a formal committal application, or thereafter by committal application, as follows:

> *"CPR 65.47*
>
> *(1) This rule applies where a person is arrested pursuant to –*
> *(a) a power of arrest attached to a provision of an injunction; or CPR 32.16;*
> *(b) a warrant of arrest.*
> *(2) The judge before whom a person is brought following his arrest may –*
> *(a) deal with the matter; or*
> *(b) adjourn the proceedings.*

(3) If proceedings under section 43 or 44 of the 2009 Act or section 9 or 10 of the 2014 Act are adjourned and the arrested person is released –

(a) the matter must be dealt with (whether by the same or another judge) within 28 days of the date on which the arrested person appears in court; and

(b) the arrested person must be given not less than 2 days' notice of the hearing.

(4) An application notice seeking the committal for contempt of court of the arrested person may be issued even if the arrested person is not dealt with within the period in subparagraph (3)(a).

(5) Sections 2 and 8 of Part 81 apply where an application is made in the County Court to commit a person for breach of an injunction as if references in those Sections to the judge include references to a district judge."

The Civil Procedure (Amendment No. 3) Rules 2020, relevant parts of which come into effect on 1 October 2020, substantially revise CPR 81. CPR 81.3 will state

"(1) A contempt application made in existing High Court or county court proceedings is made by an application under Part 23 in those proceedings, whether or not the application is made against a party to those proceedings. (2) If the application is made in the High Court, it shall be determined by a High Court judge of the Division in which the case is proceeding. If it is made in the county court, it shall be determined by a Circuit Judge sitting in the county court."

Sentencing

The court may either impose an unlimited fine or a sentence of imprisonment for up to two years: s.14(1) Contempt of Court Act 1981. There is no tariff for 'sentences' for contempt of court. It is entirely a matter for the judge and every case must inevitably depend upon its own facts: *Longhurst Homes Ltd v Killen [2008] EWCA Civ 402 (unreported) per* Hughes LJ (as he then was) at [14].

There are three main objectives in sentencing for contempt of court:

    a.   Punishment for breach of the court order;

    b.   Secure future compliance;

    c.   Rehabilitation of the tenant/s.

Rehabilitation of the tenant/s is more likely in the event of a breach by a hoarder. It is likely, however, that an ASBI would not have been imposed in the first place because of the nature of hoarding and that the hoarder is unlikely to understand the consequences were he or she to breach.

Solihull v Willoughby [2013] EWCA CIV 699, [2013] HLR 36

The committal order should reflect the aggravating and mitigating features of the breaches. Aggravating features will include deliberate flouting of the court's order on repeated occasions and breach of a suspended order for imprisonment. Mitigating features may comprise personal inadequacy (as is most likely the case with hoarding cases) admissions of breach, a low level of anti-social behaviour (such as hoarding) and efforts to reform (engagement with mental health services and/or social services to get to the root cause of the hoarding and come up with methods of management and control): *Solihull v Willoughby* at [20].

In *Amicus Horizon v Thorley [2012] EWCA Civ 817; [2012] HLR 43* it was held, at [5], [9], and in *Doey v LB Islington [2012] EWCA Civ 1825; [2013] H.L.R. 13* (*per.* Jackson LJ at para. 3). that in sentencing a defendant for breach of the terms of an anti-social behaviour injunction made under the Housing Act 1996, the court should consider the guidance issued by the Sentencing Guidelines Council ('the guidelines') in relation to breaches of anti-social behaviour orders made under the Crime and Disorder Act 1998. This does not however apply to repeat offenders: *Solihull v Willoughby* at [23].

The Guidelines provide the following important principles:

    a.   The main aim of sentencing for breach of a court order is to achieve the purpose of the injunction order (p. 2, para. 6);

    b.   The sentence for breach of an order must be commensurate with the seriousness of the breach (p. 2, para. 7) and must be assessed with reference to culpability. Culpability has two aspects (p. 3, para. 11):

    i. The degree to which the offender intended to breach the order: this includes recklessness as to whether the order was breached or whether the offender was aware of the risk of breach (one must be careful to confuse recklessness as to the impact of the order and breach with an unwariness and lack of ability to understand by virtue of their hoarding disorder);

    ii. The degree to which the offender intended to cause the harm that resulted or could have resulted (very likely low in hoarding cases given the nature of the disorder).

c. Seriousness must take into account not only the harm actually caused by the breach but also any harm that was intended or might foreseeably have been caused (p. 3, para. 13);

d. The original conduct that led to the making of the order is a relevant consideration insofar as it indicates the level of harm caused and whether this was intended (para. 4, para. 15).

It is not necessary to show that the person had a wilful intention to disobey a court order (as is often the case in hoarding) but merely that he or she knew what he or she was doing was prohibited and would lead to imprisonment or arrest: *P v P (Contempt of Court: Mental Capacity) [1999] 2 FLR 897*. This can be tricky in hoarding cases because much of the time, they do not even know that what they are doing may cause harm to others in addition to themselves. Of more general relevance is Practice Direction (Committal for Contempt: Open Court) [August 2020].

CHAPTER SEVEN
HOARDING AND
POSSESSION

This chapter considers the different grounds for seeking possession and the types of notices depending on the ground and type of tenancy.

When might possession be necessary?

Hoarding creates a risk to the health and safety of the hoarder and neighbours as well as anyone who may come into contact with the property, such as contractors or the emergency services.

Often the consequences of hoarding is that the hoarder and the people that live with the hoarder are living in unsanitary conditions, cluttered conditions and at times living in such cluttered conditions that the occupier/s are unable to clean These properties are often susceptible to infestation by rats, insects and other unwanted guests.

Fire hazards and fire risks are greater in hoarders' properties because the items hoarded are combustible and/or there is no accessible fire escape route. As a result, landlords, including local authorities and housing associations, face being accused of not fulfilling its statutory duties. Pursuant to section 36(2) Part F of the Gas Safety (Installation and Use) Regulations 1998, refusing access or making it physically impossible for gas inspections is a failure to comply with the statutory duty therein.

The cost/s of retuning the property/ies to the landlord or local authority or housing association can be significant and potentially in breach of the Decent Home Standard (for social landlords). This is because the hoarding has been such that the hoarding has prevented the property from being maintained and/or cared for. Should the occupier die or abandon a property that includes items hoarded, it can also prove costly to clean and remove the same.

Statutory basis

Should an injunction not be successful, an applicant landlord, housing association or local authority, may wish to seek possession.

Serious hoarding may represent a clear breach of the tenancy agreement to either keep the property in a good state of repair, or to allow access for required works. One may be evicted under either Ground 1, Schedule 2 of the Housing Act 1985 (for secure tenancies) or Ground 12, Schedule 2 of the Housing Act 1988 (for assured tenancies). The hoarder is likely to be evicted and would have to clear the property at their own expense.

Notice – Assured Shorthold Tenancies

When seeking to serve a notice on the basis of fault, the appropriate notice is a section 8 notice. This must be in the prescribed form. For Assured Shorthold Tenancies and Assured Tenancies, this is contained in Schedule 1 to the Assured Tenancies and Agricultural Occupancies (Forms) (England) Regulations 2015 SI no 620 regulation 2.

Any notice that is not served on the correct prescribed form will be invalid unless it is in form substantially to the same effect, see *Mannai Investment Co Ltd v Eagle Star Life Assurance [1997] UKHL 19; [1997] AC 749; [1997] 3 All ER 352; [1997] 2 WLR 945*. If the notice paraphrases the information required, this is likely to be considered as substantially to the same effect.

The notice must state on it 'Notice of Seeking Possession' and the statutory reference is also important. This is so the tenant knows where to look in statute for the power/s relied on by the landlord. If there are joint tenants, the notice must be served on all of them, even if some of the tenants no longer occupy the property. The notice must specify the ground/s relied on. The words should set out the substance of the ground if not all the words of the relevant ground(s) is included.

There is a part of the notice which has a section permitting the landlord or agent or officer to expand. This sets out what the complaint is, the particular facts, albeit in brief, and the way/s in which the tenant/s may be able to remedy the cause/s for possession being sought. Hoarding would likely fall within the nuisance ground. Pursuant to *Camden LBC v Oppong [1996] 28 HLR 701, CA* at [703] the Court of Appeal emphasised that simply describing the various acts of nuisance or instances of dilapidation would be insufficient. Explaining the impact would be of benefit. Repeating the statutory ground/s in the particulars is also insufficient.

A notice must include the date before proceedings may not be issued and the date after which proceedings may not be issued. The latter date must be 12 months from the date of service of the notice. The dates given depends on the ground/s relied on. The likely relevant grounds under the Housing Act 1988 is Ground 14 (nuisance). The date for this ground is the date on which it is served. This means that proceedings can be issued as soon as the notice has been served, see section 8(4).

The landlord must prove that the notice has been served. Even though it is not uncommon for one to send a notice by first class post, it is only if the tenant is personally served that a landlord can be certain of service. A landlord cannot prove that the notice has come to the attention of the tenant using other methods.

Occasionally the court will allow the notice to be dispensed with providing it does not concern grounds 7A or 8 (pursuant to the Housing Act 1988), and if it is just and equitable to do so (section 8(1)(b) and (5)). Such discretion is exercised rarely and only in exceptional cases, see *Braintree DC v Vincent [2004] EWCA Civ 415*.

Notice – Assured Fixed Term

If the landlord is a social landlord and there is an assured fixed term tenancy, it too must serve a notice under section 8 of the Housing Act 1988. The same principles aforesaid apply, except that for grounds 6 and 7 it cannot recover possession until the fixed term has come to an end.

Notice –secure periodic tenancies pre-Housing and Planning Act 2016

The notice must, if served based on the grounds in Schedule 2 of the Housing Act 1985, must meet the requirements of section 83 of the Housing Act 1985. It must also be in the correct prescribed form contained in the Secure Tenancies (Notices) Regulations 19887 SI o 755, as amended by the Secure Tenancies (Notices) (Amendment) (England) Regulations 1997, SI no 71 and subsequent Secure Tenancies (Notices) (Amendment) (England) Regulations 2004, SI no 1627, and the Secure Tenancies (Notices) (Amendment) (Wales) Regulations 2005, SI No, 1226. The form must be substantially to the same effect if not identical to the form prescribed. As with section 8 notices it must specify the ground/s relied on and the names of the tenant/s (even if no longer occupying). As with section 8 notices, the particulars must set out what is being relied on (other than a verbatim rendition of the statutory grounds).

The specified date must be no earlier than the date on which the tenancy (or licence as the case may be) could have been brought to an end by a notice to quit or notice to determine given by the landlord on the same date that the notice seeking possession is served, see sections 83(3) and (5) of the Housing Act 1985. Unlike the Housing Act 1988, the court cannot amend the dates, though it is rare for such power to be exercised in relation to tenancies falling under the Housing Act 1988 in any event. The notice must also state that it ceases to be in force 12 months after the date so specified.

As with section 8 notices, the court may dispense with a section 83 notice but not a section 83ZA notice.

If the landlord relies on an absolute ground for possession, the procedure is set out at section 83ZA of the Housing Act 1985.

Given that in a case of hoarding one may have breached a criminal behaviour order under the Anti-Social Behaviour, Crime and Policing Act 2014 and/or has committed an offence under sections 80(4) or 82(8) of the Environmental Protection Act 1990, the notice, in that event, must also state the conviction relied upon and must be served on the tenant within the period of 12 months beginning with the date of the conviction or, if the conviction is being appealed, the period of 12 months from the date of the beginning of when the appeal was finally determined (or discontinued).

If relying on condition 2 of (breach of an ASBI), then the notice for possession thereto must also state the findings on which the landlord seeks to rely and be served on the tenant within 12 months beginning on the date on which the court has made the finding/s or, there that is appealed, the date on which the appeal is determined or discontinued.

If relying on conditions 3 (closure order made under section 80 of the Anti-Social Behaviour Act 2014), the notice must state the closured order in question and must be served within 3 months from the date of the order or, if appealed, from the date the appeal is determined or discontinued.

Occasionally tenants of local housing authorities may seek a review of the reason/s given for the notice served pursuant to section 84A. The review procedure regime is found in the Absolute Ground For Possession for Anti-Social Behaviour (Review Procedure) (England) (Regulations) 2014, SI no 2554 and, in Wales, the Absolute Ground For Possession for Anti-Social Behaviour (Review Procedure) (Wales) (Regulations) 2014, SI no 3278. If an oral hearing has been requested by the tenant/s, then the date, time and place of the oral hearing should be given to the tenant/s and not be heard earlier than five days (ten days in Wales) after the date on which the notice of the hearing is received by the tenant. The review is conducted by anyone appointed by the landlord so long as they were not involved in the original decision.

At the oral hearing, representations can be made and questions can be put to anybody giving evidence at the hearings. The decision thereafter must be made in writing and include the reasons for it.

Notice – fixed term tenancies pre- Housing and Planning Act 2016

In addition to using section 83, 83ZA or 83A, the landlord must also ensure that the tenancy agreement contains a provision for it to determine the fixed term before its expiry. Thereafter, there are options to end the term:

a. Obtain a possession order;
b. Obtain an order under section 82(3) (this means the court may terminate the fixed term where it would otherwise have been brought to an end by a provision for re-entry. This is subject to section 146 of the Law of Property Act 1925 on forfeiture) or
c. Obtain a demotion order under section 82A.

Notice – Secure tenancies post Housing and Planning Act 2016

This arises where seeking to bring to an end a tenancy during the fixed term under any of the statutory grounds for possession, and at the expiry of the fixed term.

The landlord may bring the fixed term and tenancy to an end by obtaining a possession order (section 82(A1), Housing Act 1985). There is no requirement to bring the fixed term to an end under section 82(3) of the Housing Act 1985 first. The requirements are the same as for serving a notice under sections 83 or 84A of the Housing act 1985 for the pre-Housing and Planning Act 2016 periodic tenancies.

Grounds for possession against assured or secure tenants

The most common grounds in hoarding cases are:

a. the anti-social behaviour ground (Ground 14, first limb, Housing Act 1988 and Ground 2, first limb, Housing Act 1985);
b. breach of tenancy conditions (Ground 12, Housing Act 1988 and Ground 1, second limb, Housing Act 1985);
c. waste or neglect ground (Ground 13 Housing act 1988 and Ground 3 Housing Act 1985);

d. neglect and/or deterioration of furniture ground (Ground 15, Housing Act 1988 and Ground 4 Housing Act 1985).

Each of these grounds are discretionary. Given the nature of hoarding, and the likely defences that may be raised, it would be uncommon and indeed highly undesirable (and unlikely to succeed) to pursue possession as against a hoarder on the basis of the mandatory ground pursuant to Ground 7A of the Housing Act 1988.

Being discretionary grounds, therefore, this means that the court will consider the reasonableness of seeking possession based on the facts before him or her of what the tenant/s is alleged to have done that falls within the remit of the relevant ground. When dealing with a public body such as a local housing authority or housing association (or charity), the court will also have additional regard for the Equality Act 2010, Human Rights Act 1998, EHCR, Wednesbury reasonableness, procedural propriety, rationality, and fairness. The considerations are akin, in such cases, as to those in a Judicial Review action.

<u>Ground 7A, Housing Act 1988 (assured tenants) and Section 84A, Condition 1, Housing Act 1985 (secure tenants)</u>

If a mandatory ground is pursued, the likely ground would be section 84A condition 1 of the Housing Act 1985 (secure tenants) and Ground 7A of the Housing Act 1988. For each, these absolute grounds would first require a finding by the county court, crown court or magistrates that there is anti-social behaviour. In hoarding, this would be in the context of an ASBI finding, and/or following committal proceedings in respect of a breach of the injunction. The landlord would need to prove the same findings again, it having already been decided. This means that trials on the basis of these mandatory grounds tend to be quicker, providing that the notice has been completed and served correctly (as above) and subject to whether there has also been a review or not pursuant to section 85ZA of the Housing Act 1985 for secure tenants.

The offence must be a serious one and was committed on or after 21 October 2014 and was one which falls within Schedule 2A of the Housing act 1985 9for secure tenants), and was not an offence is triable only summarily.

Ground 14, first limb, Housing Act 1988 (assured tenants) and Ground 2, first limb, Housing Act 1985 (secure tenants)

Hoarding may constitute anti-social behaviour because of the lack of hygiene, pests and/or harm it causes not just to the occupier/s but to the locality and surrounds including neighbours and the wider public.

Hoarding, at its extreme, may also constitute a breach of the tenancy agreement which enables the landlord to also rely on Ground 1, second limb of the Housing Act 1985 (secure tenancies) or Ground 12 of the Housing Act 1988 (assured tenancies).

> *"The tenant or a person residing in or visiting the dwelling-house—*
>
> *(a) has been guilty of conduct causing or likely to cause a nuisance or annoyance to a person residing, visiting or otherwise engaging in a lawful activity in the locality..."*

The ground is such that the tenant/s are responsible for not only their action/s but also that of any others that live with them and/or visitors to the property. It is applicable even in cases where the tenant does not know that the visitor or other occupier is causing a nuisance or where, if they had known, he or she would not have been able to stop it, see *Portsmouth CC v Bryant (2000) 32 HLR 906, CA*. The conduct need not be deliberate. There is also no requirement for one to be culpable, see by way of example *Kensington and Chelsea RLBC v Simmonds [1997] 29 HLR 507, CA* where the Court of Appeal confirmed that there need not be fault on the part of the tenant.

One may attempt in defence to argue that the occasional visitor, and one that is uninvited, is not 'visiting the dwelling house'. Someone may also cause a nuisance or annoyance after being told they are not welcome and/or the occupier may be labouring under a physical or mental disability that prevents them from being able to turn someone away, invited or not. Such defences are often couched in terms of the Equality Act 2010 and/or Wednesbury reasonableness. Such defences have been attempted in cases such as *Croydon LBC v Moody [1999] 31 HLR 738, CA* but the court took the view that the conduct was also a breach of the tenancy agreement (Ground 1). There is no reference to 'guilt' in Ground 1. The landlord also relied on Ground 2.

Such defences and their efficacy are fact specific and what weight is given to them is entirely dependent on the quality of the evidence.

Further, one must be careful not to push such defences too much because one of the factors considered to suspend possession on terms (see below) is whether nuisance would be repeated. If the problem will still remain by virtue of one labouring under a disability, for example, and the underlying cause/s cannot be remedied, then the individual is be set up to fail and breach that suspended possession order. Should any arrest/s be made, it is not itself indicative of anti-social behaviour and/or nuisance and judges are encouraged to be slow to conclude the same.

'Nuisance or annoyance likely to cause'

These words are given their ordinary, natural meaning. They are not confined to the legal definitions typically found for public and private nuisance. Examples include anything likely to trouble the ordinary sensible person/s even if there is no physical interference, see Bowen LJ in *Tod-Heatly v Benham [1988] 40 ChD 80* at [98]. There may be more than act/s or an isolated. An isolated incident must be serious to be considered sufficient to trigger the ground. With hoarding, it could be the smells, the rubbish, the pests, the structure of a block of flats or the noise relating to the possessions hoarded themselves which constitutes a nuisance or annoyance. With hoarding, there is s difficult balance that must be struck between the protection of those in the locality and the right/s of the tenant to live, uninterrupted, with possession/s of their choosing that are not in and of themselves illegal.

Witness statements and a properly particularised Particulars of Claim, often with the assistance of a schedule like a Scott Schedule, is helpful.

The nuisance and/or annoyance itself may not necessarily involve an actual victim. It is enough that the conduct and evidence of the same was likely to cause such annoyance and/or nuisance. Generally, the victims tend to involve neighbours but the Ground extends to others living in, visiting or otherwise properly conducting themselves in the locality. *Manchester City Council v Lawler [1999] 31 HLR 119, CA* highlighted that what constitutes 'locality', like the conduct itself, is fact specific. There is no one catch all definition.

The fuse, if you like, tends to be longer with social landlords because of the likely defences that might be raised, including the question of what is reasonable. Unfortunately for victim/s and/or the locality, one cannot compel the landlord to act, see *Hussain v Lancaster City Council [1999] 31 HLR 164, CA* by way of example.

Reasonableness – in nuisance/annoyance cases

It is for the landlord to prove that it is reasonable that an outright possession of the tenant's home be ordered, see section 85A(2) of the Housing Act 1985 (secure tenancies) and section 9A of the Housing Act 1988 (assured tenancies).

In determining the reasonableness, and whether to suspend and/or stay (on terms) a possession order or eviction if possession is granted the court is asked to consider:

a. the effect that the nuisance or annoyance has had on persons other than the person against whom the order is sought;
b. any continuing effect of the nuisance or annoyance is likely to have on such persons; and
c. the effect that the nuisance or annoyance would be likely to have on such persons if the conduct is repeated.

All relevant circumstances must be considered, see *City West Housing Trust v Massey and Others [2016] EWCA Civ 704* at [61]. The court should be invited to consider, among other issues:

a. The seriousness and frequency of the nuisance;
b. Whether it is continuing, persistent or recently abated, see *Barking & Dagenham LBC v Bakare [2012] EWCA Civ 750; [2012] HLR 34* at [24];

c. The likelihood of the nuisance continuing or re-occurring, see *City West Housing Trust v Massey and Others [2016] EWCA Civ 704* at [49]. With hoarding the court must be live to the fact that hoarding is not necessarily within one's control until such time when they receive much needed help. This is where practitioners are encouraged to be well versed in hoarding before making such submissions because not all judges will have come across hoarding and/or appreciate the severity of it and that is recognised as an illness/disability (see Chapter 1). This does not mean that this gives the court green light to grant outright possession, and particularly if there is an underpinning disability/ies causing the same and/or steps to assist the individual/s have not been taken so far. This sometimes means that the court will suspend on terms that they comply if there is an assurance of that person/s receiving help to prevent the hoarding from getting any worse and/or arrange for the hoarding to be brought under control: *"always be a sounds basis for the hope that the anti-social behaviour will cease" (Canterbury CC v Lowe [2001] 33 HLR 53, CA)*. This is often weighed up against the interest of the neighbours and locality, but regard is also had for the risk of the hoarding merely moving to somewhere else. It is a difficult balance with the Equality Act section 149 duty concerning the public sector equality duty;

d. Warnings issued by the landlord;

e. The tenant/s remorse and genuine efforts made, see *Greenwich LBC v Grogan [2008] EWCA Civ 1315* at [26];

f. Relevant personal circumstances of the tenant/s;

g. The consequences of making an outright possession order on the tenant/s, see *Darlington BC v Sterling (1997) 29 HLR 309, CA* at page 316;

h. Consider any medical evidence of the tenant's physical and/or mental health and consider if, with treatment, the behaviour could continue (in the event of hoarding, trying to work on the collaborative measures set out in Chapter 2), *see Croydon LBC v Moody [1999] 31 HLR 738, CA.*

The court should also consider whether alternative remedies have been considered and executed, and whether these are set out in the landlord's policy (if a housing association, charity or local housing authority), see

Barber v Croydon LBC [2010] EWCA Civ, [2010] HLR 26 at [44] and [46].

The court can also consider whether there have been further allegations of nuisance up until trial, see *Wandsworth LBC v Hargreaves [1995] 27 HLR 142 CA* by way of example at pages 148 and 149.

Substantive guidance is set out in *Manchester City Council v Higgins [2005] EWCA Civ 1423; [2006] HLR 14* at [35-38]:

> *"35. First, the discretion is quite unfettered save that, of course, it must be judicially exercised. It follows that all the circumstances of the case are material to be borne in mind. In one case the facts giving rise to the making of an ASBO may be so serious that both the making a possession order and the refusal to suspend it will be self evident. In another case the making of the ASBO may have served its purpose of restraining future misbehaviour so that although past conduct might make it reasonable to order possession yet suspension might still be possible.*
>
> *36. Secondly, if the misconduct by the tenant or even by a member of the household were serious and persistent enough to justify an ASBO then that will be strong but not conclusive evidence that the tenant will have forfeited his entitlement to retain possession. As Robert Walker L.J. observed in West Kent Housing Association Ltd v Davies (1998) 31 H.L.R. 415, 425 the judge must not underestimate: "the effect both on the neighbours ... and other parts of the estate and on the housing association itself of the message that is given if serious breaches ... occur and the court, on the matter being taken to it, makes no order against tenants who are found to have committed those breaches." As Simon Brown L.J. put it in Portsmouth CC v Bryant (2000) 32 H.L.R. 906, 913: "It would in my judgment be quite intolerable if they [the neighbours] were to be held necessarily deprived of all possibility of relief in these cases, merely because some ineffectual tenant next door was incapable of controlling his or her household." Kay L.J. said this in Canterbury CC v Lowe (2001) 33 H.L.R. 53: "There is a need to support those who do have the courage to come forward and complain when complaint is legitimate about their neighbours in this sort of way."*

Waller L.J. added: "The housing association has, it seems, been doing its best to improve the quality of life for those living on this estate. To take a matter like this to court calls for considerable effort and determination on the part of a socially responsible landlord, in marshalling a case, and in obtaining witnesses who are prepared to give evidence despite the possibility of intimidation. It cannot to my mind be right that the court should not recognise the seriousness of a case of this sort."

37. Thirdly, since the court will already have found that it is reasonable to make a possession order, the question of whether or not to suspend its execution must be very much a question of the future. As Kay L.J. held in Canterbury CC v Lowe: "There is no point suspending an order if the inevitable outcome is a breach. Any factor which is relevant as to whether there will be future breaches must, in my judgment, be relevant to the question of suspension. This would include the fact that following an injunction things had considerably improved or that a person is likely to observe an injunction if one was granted at the same time." Previous unheeded warnings point one way: genuine remorse the other. The level of support available to a parent who is making proper efforts to control an errant child will be relevant. There must, however, always be a sound basis for the hope that the anti-social behaviour will cease.

38. Ultimately, given the Art.8 ECHR respect for the tenant's home, the question is whether an immediate possession order is necessary in order to meet the need to protect the rights and freedoms of others— the neighbours—and is proportionate to it."

The Court also held in *London Borough of Lambeth v Debrah [2007] EWCA Civ 1503* that, while section 85A applies to the making of the order, in considering a stay, the judge's discretion under section 85(2) is unfettered. However, the Court of Appeal held in *Manchester City Council v Higgins [2005] EWCA Civ 1423* that it should be exercised with particular reference to the future. Section 85A considerations apply to the making of the possession order under statute, as well as to the question of a stay or suspension.

Ground 12, Housing Act 1988 (assured tenants) and Ground 1, second limb, Housing Act 1985 (secure tenants)

The court must first consider whether the breach relied on was an obligation set out in the tenancy, whether express or implied. With hoarding the condition or term tends to be one of keeping the property in a habitable condition and ensuring that it is no greater than reasonable wear and tear in terms of any damage in the property (whether caused by hoarding and/or general living and going about one's day to day business of living therein).

Another common provision is one of not keeping pets or other animals in or on the premises. For those that are animal hoarders this is an obvious example of a breach of a term of the tenancy. If, however, one does not display the signs of animal hoarding and has an animal as a companion, for example, or has an animal for medical reasons, then the likelihood of them being evicted for this is slim. If they have been given notice to get rid of the animal, on the other hand, and/or move to another property where they can have their animal, then possession will likely be granted should they then fail to do so, see by way of example *Green v Sheffield City Council [1994] 26 HLR 349, CA*.

When considering whether to seek possession, therefore, on the grounds of a breach of the term/s about keeping pets and/or animals, first consider if the number/s is such as to constitute animal hoarding and/or on interviewing the tenant and/or observing their lifestyle it becomes apparent that they are showing signs of hoarding animals. Second, consider if there are other more collaborative measure/s that can be taken to assist the hoarder to deal with the root cause. Third, consider the impact of the animal hoarding continuing as against the impact on the locality pursuant to the Equality Act 2010 section 149 while keeping in mind the issue of potential indirect disability discrimination under section 15 of the Equality Act 2010 and the welfare of the animal.

Being a discretionary ground, it is subject to what is reasonable (as above).

Ground 13 Housing Act 1988 (assured tenants) and Ground 3 Housing Act 1985 (secure tenants)

This usually concerns deterioration to the common parts which is defined in section 116 of the Housing Act 1985 (and Housing Act 1988 Schedule 2 ground 13) as

> *"any part of a building comprising the dwelling-house and any other premises which the tenant is entitled under the terms of the tenancy to use in common with the occupiers of other swellin0houses let by the landlord"*

Hoarders may use the stairwells, lifts, bin stores etc as an extension of their property to hoard more items belonging to them. This may cause the common areas, and not just their property, to become unsightly, smelly, worn or even unusable by other residents, in addition to being a potential fire hazard and/or trip hazard and/or preventing the escape route in the event of a fire. The court will benefit from seeing before and during tenancy pictures to see that the tenant/s in question are indeed the culprits. CCTV is often helpful in common areas for such purposes. Being a discretionary ground, it is subject to what is reasonable.

Ground 15, Housing Act 1988 (assured tenants) and Ground 4 Housing Act 1985 (secure tenants)

This is the same as aforesaid except that it does not include furniture in the common parts. It also includes damage caused by visitors.

Reasonableness – generally – section 7(4) Housing Act 1988 and section 84(2)(a) Housing Act 1985 (secure tenants)

It is possible to argue that the landlord failed to engage other agencies such as the community mental health team or social services. It might be that the landlord has gone straight for the jugular without having considered other options first like an ASBI. This is more likely to be argued, and successfully, where the landlord is a housing association or local housing authority because they more than likely have a policy setting out the various steps to be taken before opting for possession. Such policies must be kept in review in cases concerning secure tenants pursuant to the

Housing Act 1996, section 218A. This does not mean to say that a failure to consider and/or opt for alternative remedies is a bar to claiming possession, and successfully.

When considering reasonableness, the following is relevant:

a. Where the tenant has committed or been convicted or a serious criminal offence in relation to the property, then unless exceptional circumstances apply, a possession order is regarded as reasonable. This is unlikely to be the case in hoarding cases;

b. Where there is an admitted breach of a covenant and absence of intention to stop the breach/es, then a possession order is regarded as reasonable. This is a likely factor that is considered in hoarding cases but then the attention turns on the cause/s and whether resolving the root of the problem would resolve the nuisance/annoyance entirely;

c. Whilst it is possible the tenant may be found intentionally homeless if evicted, this should not play on the judge's mind, see *Bristol CC v Mousah [1998] 30 HLR 32*;

d. If the tenant is personally culpable, possession in such circumstances is more reasonable, see *Royal Borough of Kensington and Chelsea v Simmonds [1996] 29 HLR 507*, at [511]. This is a likely in hoarding cases;

e. It is necessary and proportionate in the public interest. This is likely to be a key factor in hoarding cases for the risk of hoarding continuing unchecked often means it can only get worse rather than better if the root cause is not addressed. Often, however, evicting someone does not resolve the problem and only means that they will start to hoard elsewhere and become the same problem elsewhere;

f. If arrested, consider if the cause/s for the arrest is the conduct complained of. This is unlikely to be applicable in hoarding cases.

Disability Discrimination Defence

<u>Section 6 – disability- Equality Act 2010</u>

Section 6 defines disability, and it is one of substantial effect that is more than minor or trivial, see section 212(1). It is a what is called a 'protected characteristic'. The Act provides that the effect of the impairment is long term if:

a. It has lasted for at least 12 months; or
b. It is likely to last for at least 12 months; or
c. It is likely to last the remaining life of the person affected, see schedule 1 para 2.

Physical and mental impairment is given their natura meaning. There is no need to prove the effect of the impairment with certain medical conditions such as cancer, see Schedule 1 para 6.

Addiction does not count as an impairment unless the addiction was originally as a result of the administration of medically prescribed drugs or other medical treatment (Equality Act 2020 (Disability) regulations 2010, regulation 3.

<u>Section 15 – Equality Act 2010</u>

This is wider and is designed to ensure that treatment which is unfavourable because of something arising in consequence of a person's disability may amount to discrimination even where the reason for the treatment is not the disability itself. This is more likely to be fined in hoarding cases if care is not taken when considering the application of the multi-agency approach and other options that can be considered before seeking possession.

In *Akerman-Livingstone v Aster Communities Ltd v Akerman-Livingstone [2015] UKSC 15; [2015] AC 1399* the Supreme Court set out the approach to be taken to discrimination defences in possession claims (in that case, disability discrimination under section 15), holding that if a tenant/s succeeds in showing that bringing possession proceedings amounts to discrimination, the court cannot make a possession order, see

[17]. Further, the substantive right to equal treatment protected by section 35(1)(b) is different from, and stronger than, the substantive right protected by Article 8 of the European Convention of Human Rights, see [25] and [56].

As Lady Hale stated at paragraph 18, there are two questions a court must ask when dealing with whether there is unfavourable treatment due to the disability in the context of housing and possession proceedings:

> "Where section 15 is raised, therefore, and assuming that the defendant is in fact disabled within the meaning of the Act, there are two key questions: (a) whether the eviction is "because of something arising in consequence of B's disability"; this was a reformulation from that in the Disability Discrimination Act 1995, intended to make it clear that where something arising in consequence of the disability was the reason for the unfavourable treatment, the landlord (or other provider) would have to justify that treatment; there was no need for a comparison with how it would treat any other person; it might have to behave differently towards a disabled tenant from the way in which it would behave towards a non-disabled tenant; and if so (b) whether the landlord can show that the unfavourable treatment is a proportionate means of achieving a legitimate aim."

This is different to 'particular disadvantage' as found in section 19. There does not need to be a causal link between the unfavourable treatment and the disability itself, only that there is a link between the treatment and something arising out of the disability. In hoarding, for example, it might be that someone suffers OCD or compulsive hoarding or other variant of hoarding but the reason for the possession claim is the accumulation of what is perceived to be rubbish causing such a nuisance that it warrants, when exercising the test of reasonableness, the eviction of the tenant/s. The cause of the hoarding, whilst a disability, need not be the link established. The hoarding is the consequence of the disability. Where no reason is given, such as section 21 notices (Housing Act 1988), then it falls to the defendant tenant(s) to show that the actual reason for seeking possession is in some way connected to the tenant(s)' disability:

> *"Discrimination can be made out if it is shown to be a cause, the activating cause, a substantial and effective cause, a substantial reason, an important factor", see Nagarajan v London Regional Transport [1999] UKHL 36, [2000] 1 AC 501.*

The defence of discrimination can also be used in response to a Notice to Quit if the connection can be made with the tenant/s' disability as reason for the notice being served and relied upon.

Section 15 cannot be relied upon as a defence if the landlord does not know or cannot be reasonably expected to know that the tenant/s has a disability. If, however, it becomes apparent after proceedings are issued, then it becomes unlawful to take steps to attempt to secure the eviction in the knowledge that the reason/s for the ground/s relied upon arise as a consequence of the disability, see section 35(1)(b). Section 35 identifies what activities would constitute discrimination in the context of management of premises.

Those relying on section 15 generally rely on section 19 as well. When doing so, as asserted in *Swan Housing Association Ltd v Gill [2013] EWCA Civ 1566, [2014] HLR 18,* it is prudent to obtain medical evidence from an expert to illustrate what the impairment is, the nature of it and its impact including the substantial and long term effect of the same on the tenant/s to carry out normal day to day activities.

When relying on such defences, it must be remembered that the burden of proof is initially on the tenant/s to show that eviction is discrimination because of something arising in consequence of a person's disability (section 136). If the tenant/s can show this, it is then for the landlord, local housing authority, charity or housing association to prove that it was not. This is when well documented notes of action/s taken, conversations with relevant and interested parties and agencies has taken place and evidence is given of efforts made to adopt a multi-agency approach.

In the context of hoarding, the unfavourable treatment must be identified, the type of hoarding, the impact of the hoarding on the tenant/s themselves and/or the cause, if known, of the hoarding, the impact possession will have on the hoarder (and the risk that they will continue to hoard elsewhere and that possession merely shifts the problem to somewhere else without addressing the cause of the hoarding). If possession is sought due to someone else's hoarding behaviour that one lives with, then the disabled person must be added to the proceedings if the Equality Act 2010 is being relied upon, see *Hainsworth v Ministry of Defence [2014] EWCA Civ 763.*

<u>Section 19 – Indirect Discrimination – Equality Act 2010</u>

Indirect discrimination is defined in section 19 of the Equality Act 2010 as follows:

> *"(1) A person (A) discriminates against another (B) if A applies to B a provision, criterion or practice which is discriminatory in relation to a relevant protected characteristic of B's.*
> *(2) For the purposes of subsection (1), a provision, criterion or practice is discriminatory in relation to a relevant protected characteristic of B's if—*
> *(a) A applies, or would apply, it to persons with whom B does not share the characteristic,*
> *(b) it puts, or would put, persons with whom B shares the characteristic at a particular disadvantage when compared with persons with whom B does not share it,*
> *(c) it puts, or would put, B at that disadvantage, and*
> *(d) A cannot show it to be a proportionate means of achieving a legitimate aim."*

'Proportionate means of achieving a legitimate aim' ('Justification')

38. In *Akerman-Livingstone v Aster Communities Ltd v Akerman-Livingstone [2015] UKSC 15, [2015] HLR 201399* the Supreme Court stated:

   a. The burden of proof is on the landlord to show that eviction is a proportionate means of achieving a legitimate aim, see [19];

   b. In possession actions generally, and in discrimination cases in particular, the role of the court is not akin to judicial review, rather the court has to undertake the proportionality exercise for itself, see [38];

c. It cannot be taken for granted that the aim of vindicating the landlord's property rights will almost invariably prevail over a tenant's right to have due allowances made for the consequences of the tenant's protected characteristic, see [31];

d. Similarly, where social housing is involved the aim of enabling the local authority to comply with its statutory housing duties might have to give way to the equality rights of a person with a protected characteristic, see [31];

e. In understanding the proportionately exercise the court should apply structured approach, asking itself, see [28]:

    i. First, is the objective sufficiently important to justify limiting a fundamental right?

    ii. Secondly, is the measure rationally connected to the objective?

    iii. Thirdly, are the means chosen no more than is necessary to accomplish the objective?

    iv. Fourthly, is the impact of the rights infringement disproportionate to the likely benefit of the impugned measure?

It is exactly because this structured approach has to be adopted when indirect discrimination has been raised that a defence under the Equality Act 2010 cannot be summarily determined.

'Proportionate means of achieving a legitimate aim' ('Justification') is also considered at *R (E) v JFS [2009] UKSC 15; [2010] 2 AC 728* at [212-214] and paras 19, 28 and 31 in *Akerman-Livingstone.*

In *Akerman-Livingstone v Aster Communities Ltd v Akerman-Livingstone* at [59] and [60] Lord Neuberger held:

> *"That does not, however, mean that a landlord whose possession claim is met with a defence to the effect that possession is being sought because of something arising in consequence of [the defendants] disability, cannot seek or obtain summary judgment for possession. Possession could be ordered summarily if the landlord could establish that (i) the defendant had no real prospect of establishing that he was under a disability, (ii) in*

any event, it was plain that possession was not being sought because of something arising in consequence of [the] disability, or (iii) in any event, the claim and its enforcement plainly represented a proportionate means of achieving a legitimate aim."

"The problem for a landlord seeking summary judgment for possession in such a case would not be one of principle, but one of practice. Each of the three types of issue referred to in the immediately preceding paragraph would often give rise to disputed facts or assessments, e g whether the defendant suffers from a physical or mental disability, whether it has led to the possession claim, and where the proportionality balance comes down. Summary judgment is not normally a sensible or adequate procedure to deal with such disputes, which normally require disclosure of documents, and oral and/or expert evidence tested by cross-examination. There will no doubt be cases where a landlord facing a section 35(1)(b) defence may be well advised to seek summary judgment, but they would, I suspect, be relatively rare."

Although the question of justification is a substantive one, the fact that the burden of proof lies on the discriminator means that a failure to show proper consideration of less discriminatory means it will be likely to mean that the treatment cannot be justified.

'Particular disadvantage when compared with...." ('Disparate impact')
Where the link is not obvious, the disparate impact may be demonstrated by other types of evidence, such as by expert evidence (Code of Practice on Services etc at para 5.14). Disparate impact is considered also in *Homer v Chief Constable of West Yorkshire [2012] UKSC 15; [2012] ICR 704* at [14] and the phrase, 'provision, criterion, practice,' is considered in the EHRC Code of Practice etc. at para 5.6 and *British Airways plc v Starmer [2005] ILR 862* [17] and [18].

When dealing with a potential disability and there is a risk that that disability, hoarding, is being relied upon as reason for seeking possession the collaborative approach in Chapter 2 should be thoroughly considered in addition to the test of reasonableness when possession is sought as set out above. If one can answer the questions raised when considering reasonableness, then the likelihood of an Equality Act defence succeeding is minimised. This is often achieved by completing a comprehensive Equality

Act assessment. Such an assessment is not compulsory but is extremely helpful.

<u>Duty to make reasonable adjustments – section 20</u>

The duty to make reasonable adjustments is set out in section 20 EA 2010 and comprises of the three requirements. The relevant requirement for present purposes is the first requirement, set out in subsection (3) *"the first requirement is a requirement, where a provision, criterion or practice of A's puts a disable person at a substantial disadvantage in relation to a relevant matter in comparison with persons who are not disabled, to take such steps as it is reasonable to have to take to avoid the disadvantage."* 'Such steps as it is reasonable to take' is set out in the Code of Practice on Services etc, (at para 7.29).

In exercising its function in relation to the tenant, a local housing authority, housing association or charity could make the following reasonable adjustments to indicate that , the tenant is not at a substantial disadvantage in relation to one without a disability:

a. arranging additional meetings with the tenant/s before serving the notice;
b. consent obtained in relation to a medical assessment to consider also the relevance of the Mental Capacity Act 2005 and/or Care Act 2014, if applicable;
c. helping a tenant be put into contact with services like icope, social services and/or HoardingUK;
d. providing support to assist the tenant/s to manage the tenancy and medical treatment, if required;
e. putting the tenant/s in touch with the local support services, including legal professionals;
f. monitoring the tenant/s medical condition/s;
g. ensuring that the tenant/s maintained regular contact with medical professionals,
h. offering accommodation that is more suitable, if the reason for the hoarding is a desire to feel more physically secure.

Public Sector Equality Duty – section 149

Section 149 (1) sets out the public sector equality duty ('PSED'), which requires that a public authority:

> *"must, in the exercise of its functions, have due regard to the need to: (a) eliminate discrimination, harassment, victimisation and any other conduct that is prohibited by or under this Act; (b) advance equality of opportunity between persons who share a relevant protected characteristic and persons who do not share it."*

The local housing authority, charity or housing association must consider the public sector equality duty and have to approach this duty with rigour and open mind, see Aikens LJ in *R Brown) v Secretary of State for Work and Pensions [2008] EWJC 3158 (Admin)* at paras [90 to 96]:

a. The public authority decision maker must be aware of the duty to have 'due regard' to the relevant matters;

b. The duty must be fulfilled before and at the time when a particular policy (in that case) is being considered;

c. The duty must be *"exercised in substance, with rigour, and with an open mind."* It is not a question of 'ticking boxes,' while there is no duty to make express reference to the regard paid to the relevant duty, reference to it and to the relevant criteria reduces the scope for argument;

d. The duty is non-delegable;

e. The duty is a continuing one;

f. It is good practice for a decision maker to keep records demonstrating consideration of the duty, including when it has asked the question of whether the tenant/s has a disability and if so, the relevance of it to the decision and/or action/s to be taken.

In *Barnsley MBC v Norton [2011] EWCA Civ 834; [2012] PTSR 56* the Court of Appeal made clear that a public authority must comply with the duty during possession proceedings (per Lloyd LJ at para 31).

The factors have been finessed in *London and Quadrant Housing Trust v Patrick [2019] EWHC 1263 (QB)* in the context of housing:

a. when a public sector landlord like a local housing authority or housing association is contemplating taking or enforcing possession proceedings against a disabled person, the landlord will be subject to the PSED;

b. the PSED is not a duty to achieve a result, but a duty to have due regard to the need to eliminate discrimination and advance equality;

c. the PSED is designed to ensure that the particular vulnerabilities of a disabled person is fully explored;

d. the landlord is not required in every case to take active steps to inquire into whether there is disability and whether it is relevant. Such a duty arises only when there is information before the decision maker which presents a real possibility that this might be the case;

e. the PSED is a matter of substance over form;

f. the PSED is a continuing duty and does not end after a possession order is granted and before it has been enforced. It is prudent to consider the consequence of the order sought. With hoarders this normally means that they will merely move the problem to somewhere else;

g. the PSED will be a relevant consideration if the landlord knew or ought reasonably to have known of the disability;

h. the court must not consider what weight the judge/s thinks should be attached to the competing factors.

It is likely that in cases of nuisance and/or annoyance, seeking possession on the grounds that the hoarding itself is anti-social behaviour, will be regarded as a justifiable housing management practice and will be a legitimate aim, see *Paragon Asra Housing Ltd v Neville [2018] EWCA Civ 1712*. Given hoarding is more complex than a mere committing of behaviour considered a nuisance and/or annoyance, it can be argued that the nuisance results from a mental health problem (hoarding disorder) and thus the tenant/s may be assisted by considering whether the provision of care, social or medical services would be sufficient to reduce or remove the nuisance so that eviction is not necessary to achieve the legitimate aim of bringing the nuisance to an end. This multi-agency approach, as explained in Chapter 2, is itself achieving a legitimate aim (resolving the underlying cause (hoarding disorder) rather than merely tackling the nuisance itself).

Human Rights

A human rights defence, whilst it can be pleaded, rarely takes a defence much further in cases of hoarding when in the majority of hoarding cases the question of what is reasonable arises (discretionary grounds being primarily what are relied upon) and/or submissions that can be made intertwine with submissions made in respect of a pleaded Equality Act 2010 defence. This does not mean to say that the ECHR and the Human Rights Act 1998 are not relevant but the submissions as to alleged interference with Article 8(2) will likely be dealt with somewhat surreptitiously with the test on reasonableness and the Equality Act 2010.

CHAPTER EIGHT
THE MENTAL CAPACITY ACT
2005 AND HOARDING

This chapter considers the test applicable when dealing with hoarders and in particular who can help when considering plans to put to the Court of Protection

Test

Under section 2(1) of the Mental Capacity Act 2005 ('MCA 2005') a person lacks capacity if:

> *"at the material time he is unable to make a decision for himself in relation to the matter because of an impairment of, or a disturbance in the functioning of, the mind or brain".*

The part of the test that states *"in relation to the matter"* is essential here because although compulsive hoarders may be able to cope with the essential legal process, they may not have insight into their behaviour and so would not be able to keep to the terms of an injunction 'IPNA') even if one were to be obtained.

Practitioners concerned with hoarding will need to be aware of what constitutes capacity because with hoarding cases, it is not unusual to find that a tenant/s does not have capacity and pursuing possession proceedings or an ASBI will fall flat without capacity having at least been assessed (and the appropriate measures put in place in litigation should issuing proceedings still be pursued).

The MCA 2005 is also relevant to those supporting a tenant and/or for those who care for them formally or informally. Such support is not confined to housing-related support services.

Section 1 – the five principles

a. a tenant must be assumed to have capacity unless it is established that he lacks capacity;

b. a tenant is not to be treated as unable to make a decision unless all practicable steps to help him to do so have bene taken without success;

c. a tenant is not to be treated as unable to make a decision merely because he makes an unwise decision;

d. an act done, or decision made, on behalf of them must be done or made in their best interests;

e. before the act is done, or the decision is made, regard must be had to whether the purpose for which it is needed can be effectively achieved in a way less restrictive of the tenant's rights and freedoms.

Section 2 – establishing lack of capacity

This is established if:

a. the tenant is unable to make a decision for him/herself in relation to a matter:
   i. because of an impairment of, or a disturbance in the functioning of the mind or brain;
   ii. it is irrelevant whether the impairment is temporary or permanent

b. it cannot be determined by mere reference to age/appearance or a condition or aspect of a tenant which might lead others to make unjustified assumptions about his or her capacity.

This is established on the balance of probabilities and the tenant must be 17 or over (unless it is an anticipatory decision), see section 18(3). Practitioners should be cautions of thinking that capacity is a single, absolute state when it is not. A tenant may have capacity when carrying out a task in the workplace but not have the capacity to confront and tidy away or clear out possessions (or animals) they have accumulated whether because they are lonely, have an emotional connection, ae a perfectionist etc. An expert would likely be needed given the complexities of hoarding. The expert will be able to determine if the tenant can comply with the relevant terms of the tenancy impacted by and/or potentially breached by the tenant as a result of his or her hoarding. Such assessments of capacity can only be achieved at the time the practitioner is being asked to make the decision.

Section 3 – inability to make decisions

Once an impairment is established, practitioners must then consider the tenant's ability to make decisions and/or understand the consequence/s of the same. To be considered unable to make decisions, this means the tenant is:

a. unable to understand the information relevant to the decision
b. unable to retain that information:
   i. ability to retain for a short period does not prevent capacity
   ii. but one must be able to keep it on-line during the decision-making process
c. unable to use or weigh the information as part of the process of making the decision
d. unable to communicate his or her decision (whether by talking, using sign language or any other means).

When carrying out the capacity test it is advised that a good record is kept of it being caried out, and that the necessary advice is taken so as to indicate evidence was considered. While a best interests decision does not have be the least restrictive option and can impinge on the human rights of a tenant, it must be objectively justified and proportionate. Pursuant to section 49 and section 1(6) regard must be had to whether the purpose for which the MCA 2005 is needed can be achieved in a way that is less restrictive of the tenant's rights and freedom of action. This is a balancing exercise and one which should be well documented for if and when permission for a plan to be put into place is sought from the Court of Protection.

Section 4 – best interest decisions

If a person is found to lack capacity, then an application will need to be made to the Court of Protection. Any decision made on the tenant's behalf, must be in their *"best interests"* (Section 1(5)).

In extreme cases, a person may need to be detained under the Mental Health Act 1983. Pursuant to section 135 an Approved Medical Health Professional may gain a warrant to enter and remove a person from the property following an assessment under section 2.

To determine what is in the best interests of the tenant, other third parties will likely need to be consulted such as doctors, carers, those with lasting power of attorney etc. Other factors or reasonable steps to consider are:

a. age, appearance or condition or aspect of behaviour which might lead others to make unjustified assumptions about what might be in the tenant's best interests (perhaps their hoarding is a cover and/or coping mechanism for something more upsetting, dark or sinister for the tenant);

b. Consider all relevant assumptions (this is decision specific, time specific and practitioners should not assume all hoarders are incompetent and/or lack capacity. Some hoarders are high functioning individuals with steady jobs and/or families);

c. All likelihood of regaining capacity and if so when that is likely to happen;

d. Encourage the tenant's participation and consider their wishes and feelings (particularly important in hoarding cases);

e. Consider the views of anyone the tenant has indicated be consulted, any lasting power of attorney or anyone else involved in his or her welfare;

f. If about life saving treatment, the decision must not be motivated to bring about his or her death.

Court Power and Court of Protection pursuant to sections 6, 16, 17 and 18 of the Mental Capacity Act 2005

Practitioners may seek an order under section 16 (2)(a) of the MCA 2005. This would have the effect of making a decision on behalf of the incapacitated tenant to make arrangements to ensure compliance with the relevant terms of the tenancy pertaining to the prevention of hoarding such as terms relating to the upkeep and maintenance of the property where reasonable wear and tear is permitted and/or terms relating to fire safety, etc.

Such is the effect of section 16 powers, it is possible that the order obtained would permit authorised contractors and/or relevant social care staff to enter the tenant's property even if they do not consent in order for the essential repair/s and/or facilitate and/or carry out the removal of fire hazards and/or possessions that are posing a danger to the health and/or safety of the tenant and/or the wider public and/or locality. The same provision and jurisdiction can be used one more than one occasion so as to continue the aforesaid authorisations and arrangements provided the tenant continues to lack capacity at the relevant time, and the best interests assessment as set out aforesaid has not altered and still justifies and/or underpins the intervention.

Section 16(2)(a) requires that whatever plan o=r arrangement is put in place, it specifies who will be involved, the relevant safeguards for protecting the welfare of the and the regularity with which this procedure, and the arrangements to which it relates, may be employed.

To seek the Court of Protection's permission, practitioners must:

a. make out a good case as to why the order is in the tenant's best interests with reference to section 4 and any assessment completed thereto including evidence of efforts made to consider the tenant's likely strong desire to be able to live independently;

b. obtain expert evidence as to why the plan proposed is in the tenant's best interests.

Applications to the Court of Protection can be made by any person with a sufficient connection with the tenant, see section 50 of MCA 2005.

A multi-agency approach is the better approach to have because the Court of Protection will need to consider what resources are available, including that of the local authority. Armed with this knowledge, the Court of Protection can then determine what is in the tenant's best interests and the plan of action, if any, that should be put in place. In hoarding the likely considerations are:

a. the need for the procedure to be carefully defined in a detailed plan. This plan must detail safeguards that will be put in place such as giving advance notice of each visit, the presence a representative from the Community Mental Health Team, the presence of a friend or close relative etc;

b. if possessions belonging to the tenant (or animals) are to be removed, the plan will need to identify to what extent and how much will be removed/ The following key questions should be asked and consider in precise terms in the plan:

    i. all of it or some of it;

    ii. will the RSCPA need to be involved;

    iii. will only possessions with no value be removed;

    iv. will possessions that are a fire hazard be the only items removed;

    v. can the possessions be kept in storage;

    vi. should it be a certain category of possessions that can be removed;

    vii. are the possessions to be recycled or disposed of.

c. if the plan considers it likely that there will be forced entry and/or that there might be resistance, the pan may incorporate involvement from the police, even if only from a distance to begin with;

Authorised agents

Regard may be had for whether there be an authorised agent. A person without capacity to understand the essence of a tenancy and the conditions attached including that they maintain the same and live in habitable condition with only reasonable wear and tear cannot be put into a tenancy by someone else unless they have special authority. It cannot be done under the doctrine of necessity or best interests because those principles afford defences, but do not convey free-standing power. The same is true of any decision made that affects how they live, including what items rubbish and possessions are retained and removed. If a tenant lacks capacity to understand that they need help in retaining a tenancy by removing their possessions and/or slimming them down, then they cannot appoint an agent to do it for them.

Capacitated tenants could agree to terms which imposed a measure of restraint upon them and their lifestyles (including what possessions they can retain or dispose of) but they would need to understand that this is what they were being asked to do. On the other hand, practitioners cannot impose restrictive measures on an incapacitated person where such restrictions may amount to restraint (unless further conditions are satisfied. This is the difficulty with tenants who are hoarders and which lack capacity and/or potential tenants who may be and/or are hoarders, and which lack capacity. Authority from the Court will be needed even if it is believed to be in a tenant's best interests.

The court approach to determine capacity in litigation

It was concluded in *Masterman-Lister [2002] EWCA Civ 1889, [2003] 1 WLR 1511, (2003) 73 BMLR 1, [2003] Lloyds Rep Med 244*, that capacity for meant capacity to conduct the proceedings (which might be different from capacity to administer a large award resulting from the proceedings). This was also the test adopted by the majority of the Court of Appeal in *Bailey v Warren [2006] EWCA Civ 51, [2006] CP Rep 26*, where Arden LJ specifically related it to the capacity to commence the proceedings (para 112). This means that capacity is to be judged in relation to the decision or activity that concerns the immediate proceeding. Lady Hale noted in *Dunhill v Burgin (Nos 1 and 2) [2014] UKSC 18* that

> *"it would have been open to the parties in this court to challenge that test, based as it was mainly upon first instance decisions in relation to litigation and the general principle that capacity is issue specific, but neither has done so. In my view, the Court of Appeal reached the correct conclusion on this point in Masterman-Lister and there is no need*

for us to repeat the reasoning which is fully set out in the judgment of Chadwick LJ" (paragraph 13).

CPR rule 21 (in requiring that a protected party must have a litigation friend):

> *"posits a person with a cause of action who must have the capacity to bring and conduct proceedings in respect of that cause of action. The proceedings themselves may take many twists and turns, they may develop and change as the evidence is gathered and the arguments refined. There are, of course, litigants whose capacity fluctuates over time, so that there may be times in any proceedings where they need a litigation friend and other times when they do not. CPR 21.9(2) provides that when a party ceases to be a patient (now, a protected person) the litigation friend's appointment continues until it is ended by a court order. But a party whose capacity does not fluctuate either should or should not require a litigation friend throughout the proceedings. It would make no sense to apply a capacity test to each individual decision required in the course of the proceedings, nor, to be fair, did the defendant argue for that"* (paragraph 15).

> *"the test of capacity to conduct proceedings for the purpose of CPR Part 21 is the capacity to conduct the claim or cause of action which the claimant in fact has, rather than to conduct the claim as formulated by her lawyers"* (paragraph 18).

CPR rule 21.3(4) offers a solution to the fact that litigation conducted in the absence of a litigation friend is ineffective. Sometimes it might be appropriate to retrospectively validate some steps but not others.

CHAPTER NINE
THE RELATIONSHIP BETWEEN THE CARE ACT 2014 AND HOARDING

This chapter considers assessments and inquiries to be undertaken when obtaining a diagnosis

Obtaining a diagnosis

A recurring theme is where a diagnosis cannot be obtained because some professionals may not recognise the DSM-5 as applicable in the UK, or even because some clinicians do not diagnose hoarding disorder because there is no treatment available in their area or at their disposal. Where that happens, no formal diagnosis of hoarding disorder will be made and consequently no hoarding-specific treatment or pathway planning is embarked on.

It may also prevent a mental capacity assessment under the Mental Capacity Act 2005 ('MCA 2005') from being carried out on the sufferer, as the diagnostic element necessary for the assessment cannot be completed. In such cases, there is nothing that would appear to prevent a capacity assessment being conducted stating that 'the individual manifests hoarding-related behaviours, diagnosis yet to be obtained' in the absence of a clinical diagnosis. However, such a statement should only be made where supporting evidence exists.

Professionals' attention can be drawn to the current ICD-11 equivalents, which may be used to formulate a diagnosis of hoarding disorder if the professional involved declines to rely on the DSM-5. A hoarding protocol developed by Islington Council contains an appendix explaining how to implement this, as well as other assessment tools and guidance aimed at individuals and professionals

Health and Wellbeing Boards

Health and Wellbeing boards (HWBs) were established under the Health and Social Care Act 2012 and are formal committees of the local authority. Their statutory duties are, in conjunction with clinical commissioning groups, to:

a. Promote greater integration in the approach to health and social care provision in its area;

b. Plan how to best meet the needs of their local population;

c. Tackle local health inequalities;

d. Produce a joint strategic needs assessment and joint health and wellbeing strategy for their local population.

There is potentially a role for local authority HWBs to consider options for the treatment of hoarding disorder, in particular through commissioning specific treatments that are available universally.

National Assistance Act 1948

The power under section 47 of the National Assistance Act 1948 permitted the removal of a person from insanitary accommodation unable to devote proper care and attention to themselves from insanitary accommodation.

This was repealed by the Care Act 2014.

Section 42 Care Act 2014 ('CA 2014')

This now requires a local authority with reasonable cause to suspect an adult:

a. has needs for care and support, or

b. is experiencing neglect and is unable to protect him/herself against that, to decide whether any action should be taken.

Under the general supervision of its Safeguarding Adults Board, such a decision must be predicated on a needs assessment, including an assessment of the impact of those needs on the person's well-being, and must take account of the person's wishes where s/he has capacity.

For any needs that are not eligible under the Care Act 2014, local authorities must provide information and advice to the individual on how those needs can be met, and how they can be prevented from getting worse (as per section 13(5)).

Sections 18 and 20 of the Care Act set out when a local authority must meet a person's eligible needs. They place duties on the local authority. If the circumstances described in the sections apply and the needs are eligible, the local authority must meet the needs in question. These duties apply whether or not business failure is at issue.

Section 19 of the Care Act covers the circumstances where care and support needs may be met for example, circumstances where no duties arise under section 18 but the local authority may nevertheless meet an adult's needs. In particular, section 19(3) permits a local authority to meet needs which appear to it to be urgent.

Hoarding assessments

The absence of a formal diagnosis of hoarding disorder does not prevent a hoarding assessment from taking place. Local authority social care and mental health teams are likely to find themselves in a position where an assessment of the hoarder will become necessary.

Although there is no definitive hoarding assessment form, the statutory threshold under section 9 of the Care Act 2014 is sufficiently low to trigger local authorities' duties to assess whether the individual may have needs for care and support.

A hoarding assessment can comprise many types of assessments or assessment tools, such as the Clutter Image Rating Scale, a local authority-specific hoarding assessment tool.

What seems clear is that the assessment cannot be any less than the statutory minimum that is necessary and relevant in such cases. It is therefore clear that a tri-partite approach will be required, involving:

a. A needs assessment under the CA 2014 to identify the person's needs for care and support;

b. A mental health assessment under the Mental Health Act 1983 in respect of the diagnosis, notwithstanding the DSM-5 versus ICD-11 debate which can potentially be resolved;

c. A mental capacity assessment for the purposes of the MCA 2005 on the specific issue as to whether the person lacks capacity to make decisions about cleaning or tidying their accommodation.

Good practice suggests that while the tri-partite assessment approach is essential, a multi-agency meeting should be convened on referral or following an alert (for example, from statutory agencies such as housing or environmental services). This would benefit the information gathering and forward planning process around the potential hoarder. The inclusion of a person's advocate or support worker should also be considered, as they will often have known the individual for a long time and can add valuable insight into what might work for them.

The multi-agency meeting could involve the police, rescue services, housing authorities, environmental health agencies, tenancy management officers, mental health workers, support workers, the referrer, social work professionals, the potential sufferer's GP or relevant clinician, cleaning services or children's services (where applicable). This list is not exhaustive but would go some way to formulating a more comprehensive picture of the often, piecemeal evidence collated about hoarders from one service in isolation to the other.

The expected bare minimum would be social care, mental health services and whichever other agency or body is involved in the particular case.

Clutter Image Rating Scale

This helps to standardise the definitions of clutter by showing images depicting rooms in various stages of clutter. It contains three sets of nine pictures to clarify the level of clutter in the kitchen, the living room, and the bedroom. The living room photos can be used to rate other types of rooms in the home. Rooms rated as picture number four or higher indicate a probable hoarding problem/diagnosis.

This scale is preferred by practitioners, but others include:

Saving Inventory-Revised ('SIR'): 23-item questionnaire designed to measure three features: excessive acquisition, difficulty discarding, and clutter. There is a table showing the average scores of people who do not suffer from hoarding disorder and cut-off points are set out therein to indicate a potential hoarding disorder.

Hoarding Rating Scale ('HRS'): five-item scale questionnaire. This includes five questions about clutter, difficulty discarding, excessive acquisition, and the resulting distress and impairment caused by hoarding. Scores of 14 or higher on indicate a probable hoarding problem/diagnosis.

MORE BOOKS BY
LAW BRIEF PUBLISHING

A selection of our other titles available now:-

'A Practical Guide to Solicitor and Client Costs – 2nd Edition' by Robin Dunne

'Constructive Dismissal – Practice Pointers and Principles' by Benjimin Burgher

'A Practical Guide to Religion and Belief Discrimination Claims in the Workplace' by Kashif Ali

'A Practical Guide to the Law of Medical Treatment Decisions' by Ben Troke

'Fundamental Dishonesty and QOCS in Personal Injury Proceedings: Law and Practice' by Jake Rowley

'A Practical Guide to the Law in Relation to School Exclusions' by Charlotte Hadfield & Alice de Coverley

'A Practical Guide to Divorce for the Silver Separators' by Karin Walker

'The Right to be Forgotten – The Law and Practical Issues' by Melissa Stock

'A Practical Guide to Planning Law and Rights of Way in National Parks, the Broads and AONBs' by James Maurici QC, James Neill et al

'A Practical Guide to Election Law' by Tom Tabori

'A Practical Guide to the Law in Relation to Surrogacy' by Andrew Powell

'A Practical Guide to Claims Arising from Fatal Accidents – 2nd Edition' by James Patience

'A Practical Guide to the Ownership of Employee Inventions – From Entitlement to Compensation' by James Tumbridge & Ashley Roughton

'A Practical Guide to Asbestos Claims' by Jonathan Owen & Gareth McAloon

'A Practical Guide to Stamp Duty Land Tax in England and Northern Ireland' by Suzanne O'Hara

'A Practical Guide to the Law of Farming Partnerships' by Philip Whitcomb

These books and more are available to order online direct from the publisher at www.lawbriefpublishing.com, where you can also read free sample chapters. For any queries, contact us on 0844 587 2383 or mail@lawbriefpublishing.com.

Our books are also usually in stock at www.amazon.co.uk with free next day delivery for Prime members, and at good legal bookshops such as Wildy & Sons.

We are regularly launching new books in our series of practical day-to-day practitioners' guides. Visit our website and join our free newsletter to be kept informed and to receive special offers, free chapters, etc.

You can also follow us on Twitter at www.twitter.com/lawbriefpub.

Printed in Great Britain
by Amazon